Nikki Riggsbee

Havanese

Everything About Purchase, Care, Nutrition, Behavior, and Training

Filled with Full-color Photographs

Illustrations by Michele Earle-Bridges

BARRON'S

CONTENTS

INTRODUCING THE HAVANESE

You are searching for a family dog that is small but sturdy, intelligent and cheerful, friendly with people, a playmate for children, and amiable with the other family pets. The Havanese might be just what you are looking for.

Description

The Havanese is small but not fragile. She has large, dark, expressive eyes that contribute to a soft, intelligent, but mischievous expression. Unlike most dogs, her back rises slightly from shoulders to rump, making her a bit taller in the rear. With her head held high and plumed tail carried jauntily over her back, the Havanese is ready to enjoy the delights of the world.

Coat: Characteristic of the Havanese is her crowning glory—her "profuse mantle of untrimmed, long, silky, wavy hair." It may be straight, wavy, or curly. The wavy coat is preferred and easiest to maintain. The coat can be up to 6 to 8 inches (15 to 20 cm) long on the body, with the leg hair shorter.

The characteristic Havanese coat comes in many colors and combinations of color.

The Havanese has a double coat, with an outer coat and an undercoat. The outer coat is longer. The undercoat is shorter, softer, and seen next to the body when the outer coat is parted. Both are soft in texture. Because of the double coat and the light texture, the Havanese coat stands off the body somewhat. This coat provides some protection from the heat, appropriate to the breed's development in the warm Cuban climate. However, the lightweight coat offers no protection against cold.

Some pet owners keep their Havanese in full show coat, usually with weekly trips to a groomer, but clip or tie the hair up out of the dog's eyes. Most pets and retired show dogs are clipped down for easier maintenance and fewer mats and tangles.

Color: The coat can be any color. Havanese come in white, shades of cream and cham-

Havanese thrive on attention from their people.

getting along well with all sorts of people and other family pets. Their merry disposition makes them excellent playmates for children.

Havanese are intelligent, eager to please, and learn tricks and commands quickly. Lively and alert, they are ready for any activity, indoors or out. Although Havanese were developed as companions and live in the house, they enjoy activity and exercise. As small dogs, they can get their exercise on walks, in a yard, or zooming around the house. They are not delicate dogs needing to be carried, pampered, or spoiled.

Havanese will bark and alert you to company coming to visit. However, they have no guarding instinct, preferring to be your visitor's new best friend. Although they will announce incoming guests, a well-bred Havanese never displays aggression, cowardice, or shyness with people or other dogs.

pagne, gold, black, blue, silver, and chocolate. They can be parti-colored, which is one color on a white or lighter background, tricolored, or even brindle (striped). The darker colors may fade and gray as the dog gets older.

Temperament

Although the unique coat and attractive size and shape have attracted admirers, the delightful temperament has won the Havanese their growing popularity. They were bred solely to be companions and well-loved pets, and their temperament is wonderfully suited to that happy task. They are people dogs, friendly and devoted to their owners. They are social and easygoing,

History

The Havanese breed is named for the city of Havana in Cuba. It is the only breed of dog native to Cuba. It is the Cuban variation of the Bichon-type lapdog that has been so popular in Europe from the Renaissance to the present day.

The Havanese is one of several related breeds in the Barbichon family. The name *Barbichon* was shortened to *Bichon*. The Bichon family of dogs was known as far back as ancient Greece. They were developed around the Mediterranean Sea, on the island of Malta, and on Tenerife, one of the Canary Islands off the northwest coast of Africa. They traveled to many lands on early trading ships during the Renaissance.

The Bichon family and the Poodle may have a common ancestor. One candidate is the poodle-like Barbet, which is a water spaniel and one of France's oldest breeds. The initial name, *Barbichon*, is a diminutive of *Barbet*, evidence of the breed's possible origin.

The small, white, Bichon-type dogs had appeared in Cuba by the early 1700s. Settlers may have brought some small dogs with them from the Canary Islands. Traders are credited with bringing the dogs to the region as gifts for wealthy Cuban women. They were popular with the island's aristocracy as ladies' lapdogs, family pets, children's playmates, and watchdogs. They also entertained as performing dogs in circuses.

As trade grew, some dogs were eventually exported back to Europe, becoming popular in England, Spain, and France in the eighteenth and nineteenth centuries. In Europe, they were called White Cubans.

Trade also brought the French and other Europeans to the Caribbean, who brought their own dogs to the islands. By the nineteenth century, Poodles had arrived in Cuba, probably brought by French and other European immigrants. Some think that the Poodle was bred with the small, white, Bichon-style dogs in Cuba, giving the varied colors we see in today's Havanese.

What's in a name? Over the years, Havanese have been called by many names, including Blanquito de la Cubano (probably an earlier white predecessor breed in Cuba), Havana Silk Dog, Habeneros, Dog of Havannah, Havana Spaniel, Toy Havanese, and Maltese, although these were not the Maltese currently recognized by the American Kennel Club (AKC). The name Havanese by itself was first used in the United States, not in its country of origin. Today in Cuba, it is called Bichon Habanero or Bichon Havanese.

TIP

Havanese Growing Popularity

In 2004, Havanese ranked 46th in popularity based on 1,273 dogs registered with the AKC, up from 56th the year before. The number of dogs registered increased over 33 percent from 2003.

Children and Havanese are natural playmates.

Havanese and related breeds evolved over centuries, although the Havanese breed was recognized by the AKC only in 1995.

Breeds Related to Havanese

	Maltese	Bichon Frise	Bolognese	Coton de Tulear	Löwchen
Weight	4–6 pounds (1.8–2.7 kg)	7–12 pounds (3.2–5.4 kg)	4.5–9 pounds (2.0–4.1 kg)	up to 15 pounds (6.8 kg)	8–18 pounds (3.6–8.2 kg)
Height	Not specified	9–11 inches (23–28 cm)	10–12 inches (25–30 cm)	up to 13 inches (33 cm)	10–13 inches (25–33 cm)
Place Developed	Malta	France	Italy	Madagascar	France
Color	White	White	White	White and other colors	Any color
Coat	Long, straight	Curly, powderpuff	Loose ringlets	Cottony, soft	Wavy
Comment	Most popular	"Frise" is French for curly.	Not yet AKC-recognized	Not yet AKC-recognized	Trimmed like a lion

By the beginning of the twentieth century, the European influence in Cuba waned as North American interests became predominant. In the early twentieth century, both in Europe and in Cuba, the breed became less the pet of the colonial aristocracy and more a companion in middle-class homes. The Cuban Revolution of 1959 was hard on the Havanese, which were closely associated with the upper and upper-middle classes and therefore no longer in favor.

In the United States: Many Cubans moved to Florida and other Central American countries in the 1960s after the revolution, and some brought their little dogs with them. Mrs. Dorothy Goodale of Colorado became interested in the breed and purchased some of the Havanese that had been brought to the United States. She found six, a female with four female offspring and another male. She later acquired five additional males that had been brought from Cuba. Eight of these original dogs are found in the pedigrees of many of the dogs in the United States today. She began breeding in the 1970s and kept a registry of the dogs bred by herself and others. In 1979, Mrs. Goodale, her husband, and other fanciers formed the Havanese Club of America (HCA). She continued to record Havanese pedigrees in the HCA breed registry.

As the Goodales and others continued breeding, the breed grew in numbers and popularity. By 1995, there was a sufficient base for the AKC to recognize the Havanese in the miscellaneous class, which is for breeds that are in process of earning full recognition. The AKC also took over responsibility for the breed registry kept by Mrs. Goodale. The Havanese recorded by the HCA were called foundation stock when the AKC took over the registry. In some pedigrees, they are still designated as such. In 1999, the AKC recognized the Havanese as part of the toy group, fully qualified to participate in all AKC activities.

All in the Family— Related Breeds

The Havanese is one of several breeds in the Bichon family of small, coated dogs. All were developed as companion animals with happy, friendly temperaments. Some are only white; others allow colors. All are comparatively odorless and have naturally long, soft, nonshedding coats. They are traditionally seen in different, sometimes unique hairstyles but may be clipped short for the convenience of an easy-care, shorter fashion. All carry their tails happily over their backs.

There's room on the couch for both you and your Havanese.

GETTING A HAVANESE

Although the Havanese is a wonderful breed and rapidly growing in popularity, it is not the right breed for everyone—no breed is. Your first big decision is determining if you and a Havanese are right for each other.

Is the Havanese for You?

When investigating a breed, you must consider many things. Your lifestyle, your home, the time you can spend with a dog, the grooming you are willing to do, and your reason for having a dog will affect your choices. The breed's characteristics may or may not suit your needs: size, temperament, grooming requirements, and energy level.

Size: The size of your home or yard is not an issue. The small Havanese does not need much space. Apartments or estates suit this breed fine. Big or small yards and neighborhood walks provide enough exercise. A small dog is an advantage if you travel and can take him. His carrier easily fits into your car or under the seat in front of you on an airplane.

All puppies are cute. Make sure a Havanese is a suitable breed for you before getting one.

Housebreaking: Small breeds tend to be harder to housebreak. If you get an adult who is already housebroken, this is not an issue. However, if you get a puppy or an adult that is not housebroken, then you have to deal with this task. It may take months of very consistent effort. You can train your Havanese to go outside. If you have a doggy door that allows him to go out when he needs to, the task is simplified. Since the dog is small, the output is also small, so you can train your dog to use a "pee pad" or a doggy litter box.

House dog: He must be housebroken, because your Havanese must live in your home, not outside, on the porch, or in the garage, even when you are not home. You may keep some rooms off limits, but your dog should be allowed into the rooms that you live in most. Your Havanese is a social dog and wants to be with you. He will get on your furniture, by the way, for he feels it is his birthright. If you do

━━━━━━━ **TIP** ━━━━━━━

Havanese Breeder Referral

The HCA provides a breeder referral list for potential Havanese buyers. To be on the list, a Havanese breeder must do the health testing required by the HCA.

not want a dog literally in the middle of your house and life and right next to you, you might prefer another breed.

Social extrovert: This is a busy breed, playful, affectionate, and entertaining. Your Havanese wants your attention and thrives on companionship. He likes people in his life as

Your Havanese will listen attentively and never tell your secrets.

much as possible. He enjoys the company of other dogs and cats, too, so a multipet home provides additional company. If you are gone all day and into the evening and all you can offer a dog is a solitary life, you might consider a breed that enjoys being alone.

Children: A Havanese is a happy playmate for children. However, if your children are younger than school age, they will need close supervision when interacting with a small dog. The younger the child, the more closely you must manage their time together to prevent accident or injury. If you do not have the time or inclination to monitor your children and dog playing together, you might wait until the children are a bit older before getting a Havanese.

Coat care: The biggest consideration in deciding on a Havanese is whether and how you will deal with his coat. It is a very soft coat that needs maintenance—possibly high maintenance, depending on the hairstyle you choose—to avoid tangles and mats. The shortest styles need the least maintenance, but you must still comb and brush it, keep it dry, and trim it regularly to keep it short. Longer styles need daily or every other day brushing, with special attention to combing and drying parts of the coat that get wet. Many people enjoy grooming their dogs as part of their personal time with the dogs. Optionally, a weekly session with a groomer will keep a long-coated dog's crowning glory resplendent. Your attending daily to the coat is part of your commitment to this breed.

On the positive side, the Havanese coat sheds minimally. It is light and soft rather than oily, so there is minimal odor from the coat. Because the dog produces less dander than many other breeds, it is considered hypoallergenic. However, if you have someone in your household who is allergic to dogs, visit Havanese homes to see if the allergies are triggered before getting a dog of your own.

Other pets: A benefit of the Havanese social nature is that he gets along with other pets. If you already have a dog or cat or two, a Havanese can join the family and get along well. However, if you have a large sighthound or an aggressive dog as a pet, you will need to manage the situation for your Havanese's safety. Some dogs will chase small, running animals. They may be friends inside the house, but some dogs may chase a small dog running in a large yard. Dog-aggressive dogs could seriously hurt a diminutive dog. On the other hand, friendly pet dogs and cats can be bonus friends for your Havanese.

Family decision: Check with all the members in your family. Getting a dog is a family decision. Are they equally enthused about getting a social toy dog? If they are not, doing so may not be a good idea. If you are really sure that this delightful breed is for you and you are willing to make a 'til-death-do-us-part commitment, now is the time to look at other decisions you need to consider.

Puppy or Adult

Most people want puppies because they are incredibly cute. You can meet the mother and other doggy family members to see what your puppy may be like when grown. Many people feel they can make a puppy into their perfect adult and not inherit someone else's problems.

However, puppies are more work than adult dogs. They need more training, socialization, and supervision. You have the big job of housebreaking to accomplish. Puppies are higher

If you keep your Havanese's coat long, it will need daily care.

energy and busier than adults of an already busy breed. Even with all your training, you will not know until he matures what he will be like as an adult. Since most people want puppies, they are usually more expensive to buy.

On the other hand, if you get an adult, you know exactly what he is like physically and in temperament and personality. You can learn if he has any issues and decide if you can deal with them before bringing him home. The adult may already be housebroken and trained. Because the breed lives for 14 to 15 years on average, you will still have many years with your adult Havanese.

You need not worry about an adult Havanese bonding with you. These friendly dogs are quite willing to make new best friends. As smart as

There are many advantages in getting an adult instead of a puppy. And Havanese adults are still incredibly cute.

TIP

Belly Bands

Boys may be harder to housebreak, and intact males may lift their legs on inappropriate objects. Belly bands—a bit like doggy diapers—are available to keep the urine from hitting its target. The belly band wraps around the dog's midsection, covering his penis, and is secured at his back. You can purchase a belly band and insert an absorbent pad. Alternatively, you can use a disposable diaper that will neatly wrap around your dog's middle.

they are, they are receptive to new training and eager to learn new tricks for you.

Adults from breeders: Reputable Havanese breeders are not only a source of puppies; they are also the first place to look for adults and teenagers. Many breeders have too many dogs, especially in long-lived breeds. She may have a retired show dog for which she would be delighted to find a great home. She may have kept a dog for herself that did not turn out to be the show dog she wanted. She may have gotten a dog back and be looking for a new forever home for him. All of these Havanese can be wonderful pets and thrive on the individual attention you can offer.

Adults from rescue: Most breeds have people involved in rescue who help find new homes for dogs that have lost theirs. A Havanese might lose his home for many reasons. They live a long time and sometimes outlive their owners. Bad things can happen to good people: health problems, divorce, job loss, having to move. Some of these events cause families to give up their dog.

Unfortunately, some people consider pets disposable and give up a dog that they no longer have time for or find inconvenient. They may have bought a Havanese on impulse. Maybe they were unwilling to housebreak the dog successfully or cope with the coat. The problem here is the previous owner, not the dog. With a little effort, an unlucky Havanese can get very lucky and be a super pet in a new home.

The HCA web site at *www.havanese.org* has a link to a rescue page if you are willing to consider providing a home to a Havanese needing a new one. They have an application you can complete. On it you tell them what you are looking for and the home you can provide as well as issues you can deal with and those you cannot.

Dogs in rescue are temporarily placed with foster families. If you are willing, you can apply (again via the HCA web site on the rescue page) to be a foster home for a Havanese in need. You would house, care for, train, and evaluate the dog until his forever home comes along. Who knows—you might become that forever home.

Male or Female

Many people feel strongly about getting either a male or a female, but either makes a wonderful pet. With Havanese, size difference is not a consideration. Each Havanese will have his or her own unique personality with few traits dictated by gender.

Certain behaviors are associated with intact dogs, those that have not been spayed or neutered. The boys may wander with loving on their minds. The girls come in season twice a year and have a vaginal discharge. These can become nonissues, if you do not intend to show or breed your dog, by neutering males and spaying females. In doing so, you also avoid some health problems that affect only intact animals.

Color

Many people seek a Havanese of a certain color or combination of colors. However, color should be your lowest priority. Buying a dog is not like buying a car; it is more like choosing a new family member. You would not select a spouse based on hair or eye color. A person's character and temperament would be more important. Discuss what you want with your breeder and let her help select the Havanese

whose personality best fits your family, regardless of color. Remember that your puppy's color may well change over his life, so there is no point in making it a priority.

Show or Pet

All Havanese are treasured pets and valued family members, whether they are exhibited at dog shows or not. Breeders will use the term "pet puppy" to identify one that is not intended to be shown or bred. So when you talk with a breeder, tell her if you want a show puppy—one that you will compete at dog shows to earn an AKC championship, or if you want a pet—one that you will not show or breed.

=== TIP ===

Pre-AKC

Dogs in the pedigree that lived prior to the AKC's recognition of the breed in 1999 may have championships from the Havanese parent club (HCA) or a rare breed organization such as the ARBA (American Rare Breed Association). Championships earned prior to AKC recognition will have an abbreviation from the organization awarding the championship, such as HCA, before the "Ch."

A serious breeder's goal is to produce the highest-quality puppies she can. The breeder will evaluate the puppies in each litter to determine which ones should be shown and used for breeding. She may keep a show puppy or sell it to someone who will show the dog to its AKC championship. The others she will place in pet homes with people who are not interested in showing.

Show Havanese are allowed only minimal trimming of their coat, and so they require much more grooming than a pet that is kept in a shorter trim. If you commit to a show dog, remember that includes a commitment to more grooming.

Every once in a while, a short-coated Havanese will be born. These cannot be shown but can make wonderful pets. Some Havanese may also be a bit bigger or smaller than desired for a show dog; these also can be excellent pets. However, do not be sold a "rare and valuable" short-coated, unusual-sized, or unusual color Havanese by unscrupulous breeders. These dogs may not be common, but they are no more valuable than any other pet Havanese.

AKC Registration

Puppies that are born to AKC-registered purebred dogs are themselves entitled to AKC registration. Show puppies are given full AKC registration, which allows them to participate in all AKC activities and, in turn, to have their puppies eligible for AKC registration.

When they sell a pet puppy, most reputable breeders want to insure that the dog will not be used for backyard breeding. If the buyers want to get involved in breeding, the breeders want to get them a show- and breeding-quality Havanese. They also want the buyers to show the dog to its championship first before breeding.

To discourage breeding of pet puppies, many breeders provide pet puppies with limited AKC registration. Limited AKC registration allows the dog to participate in all AKC events except conformation dog shows. Further, if a dog with limited registration has puppies, those puppies cannot be registered with the AKC.

Other breeders require that pet puppies be spayed or neutered and provide the AKC papers only when they get confirmation that the dog has been altered. If you get a puppy under such circumstances, make sure that when you get the puppy you also get the AKC numbers of both the sire and dam and the litter registration number. Some unscrupulous breeders breed dogs that are not purebred and not AKC registered, and they promise registration papers that never materialize.

Other good breeders spay and neuter their pet Havanese puppies before placing them into their new homes. They will provide you with the AKC papers when you get the puppy.

Both male and female Havanese make equally good pets.

The Breeder

Havanese puppies are irresistibly cute, and the popularity of the breed is growing. As a result, many people are breeding dogs who should not take advantage of the burgeoning market. Take care to consider puppies only from reputable breeders. To do otherwise may be a very expensive mistake, resulting in future problems. Getting a Havanese is not an impulse decision. Do your homework, and find a reputable breeder from whom to get your puppy.

Reputable Breeders

Reputable breeders are the best source for good Havanese puppies because their primary motives are the welfare, improvement, and advancement of the Havanese breed. They breed dogs as a hobby and are also called *hobby breeders*. They select the highest-quality dogs to breed and then retain the best puppies in each litter to be the parents of the next generation.

Reputable breeders are also the best source of information about Havanese. They can tell you from personal and extensive experience what the breed is like and what their particular family of dogs is like. They are available during the life of your dog to answer questions, provide breed-specific tips, and help with problems.

Reputable breeders are also always there for the dogs they produce. If a puppy buyer cannot keep her dog at any age and for any reason, the responsible breeder will take the dog back and either keep it or find it a new good home. Because they are willing to do this, responsible

Color should be the least important criteria when selecting a puppy. Color will likely change and fade through the Havanese's life.

breeders carefully screen prospective puppy buyers. Not only do they want wonderful homes for their puppies, but they also want people who will commit to the dog for life.

Serious breeders compete: Most serious Havanese breeders are members of the HCA if they live in the United States or of their country's Havanese parent club if they live elsewhere. They compete in conformation dog shows to compare their dogs with other breeders' dogs.

You should expect to find many champions in your puppy's pedigree. A champion has "Ch" in front of his name. Verify from the breeder that these are AKC champions (or the equivalent in other countries), because other groups offer "championships" that can be easily acquired by lower-quality animals. One or both of the puppy's parents should be champions. At least half of his grandparents should be champions, also.

Some breeders will use the term "champion lines." This means that somewhere in the pedigree, usually many generations ago, are a few champions. It usually means these puppies are lower quality and not produced by serious breeders. Others advertise "AKC" puppies. Even though top-quality puppies are definitely AKC registrable, so are poor-quality puppies as long as both of their parents were registered with AKC. Now you know and will not be misled by such terms.

TIP

HCA Health Tests

The HCA recommends health tests on eyes (CERF test), hearing (BAER test), hips, and patellas (knees). Some breeders do additional tests, including for liver shunts and heart problems.

If you are interested in competing in performance events with your Havanese, you might look for those titles on dogs in the pedigree. CD, CDX, and UD indicate AKC obedience titles. Many titles are available in agility, depending on the expertise of the dog, difficulty of the course, the obstacles used, and the agility organization putting on the competition. Some AKC agility titles include NA, NAJ, OA, and OAJ.

Reputable breeders do health checks on their breeding stock and puppies for conditions that sometimes occur in the breed. They do not want to have or propagate health problems. You do not want to deal with the health problems either, so seek a breeder who does health tests.

Why you should care: You just want a pet. Why should you care about reputable breeders and champion pedigrees? You want them because you will be spending a lot of money on this dog, and you should get the quality you are paying for. This dog will be part of your family for 15 years or more. You want it to be healthy and have a good temperament. You want access to reliable help and information that only a reputable breeder will provide.

So . . . Where Are the Good Breeders?

First consider where reputable breeders are not. With the popularity of the Havanese, many people are breeding them whose primary goal is money, and they will sell their puppies to anyone who can pay for them. Commercial breeders and puppy mills are not sources of good puppies. Backyard breeders with little knowledge of the breed and with poorer-quality dogs are not good sources either. Such breeders

TIP

How Old Will Your Puppy Be

Although a puppy can leave its litter at eight weeks, many Havanese breeders keep their puppies for 10 to 12 weeks. One reason is to evaluate the quality of the puppies better. Another is to provide very important early socialization for the youngsters.

often use flea markets, auctions, or newspaper ads to sell puppies. Many use the Internet as well. Beware of big-time advertising, for the

An exhibitor waits with her Havanese for their turn to compete in the dog show ring.

A Havanese breeder shows her dog to compete for his AKC championship.

best breeders seldom advertise since people already want their puppies.

The HCA web site at *www.havanese.org* is a good place to find reputable breeders. Click on *Breeder Referral* to get a contact who can help you find a Havanese breeder. The *Local Club* link provides information to find representatives from Havanese clubs across the country. Although the site does not include a list of all their members, it does include lists of officers, board members, and committee chairs who may also help you find breeders who are members of HCA.

At dog shows: Another excellent place to find reputable breeders is a local dog show. You can find shows in your area on the AKC's web site at *www.akc.org*. Click on *Events* and then *Event and Awards Search*. Specify a time period and your state, and click *Search*. You will get a list of shows, their locations, and the event dates. If you click on the show link, you will find more data plus whom to contact for further information, often the show superintendent who will help put on the show.

About a week before the show, visit the superintendent's web site to find the judging schedule for the show specifying the ring and time where the Havanese will be shown. At the show, you can visit the owners, breeders, and handlers with Havanese and arrange future visits to get to know the people and their dogs. Remember that although they look casual, the dogs have been carefully groomed for the show. Ask before you pet any dog; owners may ask you to wait until after a dog has finished in the ring before you pet him.

Evaluating a Havanese Breeder

More important than picking a specific dog is picking your breeder. Your dog will be a product of your breeder's efforts. You will have a significant investment in emotion, money, and time in this dog, so the breeder is paramount. You will have a relationship with your breeder for the life of your dog. So what should you look for?

The breeder with the most dogs, who lives closest to you, or who has the flashiest web site may not be your best choice. Look for breeders who are members of the HCA. Consider only breeders who register their dogs with the AKC (or the equivalent in other countries). The AKC is the most reliable registry and is the only non-profit registry in the United States. Other registries created primarily for commercial breeders do not have AKC standards. If a breeder explains that she does not register with the AKC because she does not show or that the AKC is expensive, look for another breeder.

Inquire about dog clubs that the breeders are members of and active in. Quality breeders

Visit breeders, meet and play with her dogs; they should be happy, healthy, friendly, and well cared for.

show their dogs, so ask about this activity. Reputable breeders breed dogs for themselves as well as to place in good homes. They, like you, want their dogs to be the best they can be in quality, structure, health, and temperament. Ask about the health tests the breeder does on her breeding stock.

Visit the breeders: Call the recommended Havanese breeders. Talk to and visit as many as you can to find the one you like best and whose dogs you like best. Meet their family of dogs. The dogs should be happy, friendly, healthy looking, and well cared for. Your puppy will resemble the breeder's dogs, not just physically but also in temperament. You can expect

to meet the puppies' mother; the father may live elsewhere. Good breeders breed their females to the best males they can find, and those may live in a different part of the country. Be suspicious of breeders who do not want you to meet their dogs

See where the dogs live; it should be clean and comfortable for the dogs. Ideally, they should be in the house and live with the family. Sit to visit with the dogs, either on the furniture or on the floor. Even friendly dogs can be intimidated when a giant—you—looms over them from above.

Questions to ask: When you talk to the breeder, tell her what you are looking for in as

Reputable breeders have invested a great deal in their dogs and puppies and are very selective about the homes they go to.

much detail as possible and ask what you can expect from a Havanese puppy. Ask about breed health issues; the breeder should be candid with you. Ask what socialization the breeder does before placing her puppies. Learn her recommendations on housebreaking and what she does before the puppies go to their new homes.

What does she recommend for puppy trims? What does she advise you to learn and do to groom your puppy? What grooming will she have done with the puppies? Review her puppy contract with her. What will she provide, and what is required of you?

Your goal is to find a reputable breeder who is knowledgeable, who breeds quality dogs, someone you are comfortable with, and whose dogs you like. That is the breeder you will want a puppy from and who will be your breed mentor for years to come.

She may not have a litter ready when you want a puppy. You will probably have to wait for your Havanese. This is not K-Mart, with lots of puppies waiting for you. (If her kennel looks like that, find another breeder.) Responsible breeders breed only puppies that they can find excellent homes for. Ask when the next litter is planned. Ask to be put onto the waiting list. Reputable breeders' puppies are in demand. Use the interim to get to know your breeder, her dogs, and the breed better. After having found the right breeder, it will be worth the wait.

Havanese puppies are all incredibly cute.

Breeders Will Evaluate You

Breeders want the very best homes for their puppies. Therefore, they will ask many questions of you to learn about you. If the breeder does not interview you or does not seem picky about where her puppies go, find another breeder.

She will want to know what dogs you have had, how you cared for them, and what happened to them. She will be interested in whether you have had toy dogs and/or coated dogs and how successful you were with housebreaking and grooming. She will want to know where in your home your Havanese will live. She will ask about the people in your family, how many are home during the day, whether you have children, and if so, how old they are. Since this is a long-lived breed, if you are a senior citizen, she may discuss what can be done if you can no longer care for the dog.

Do not be insulted by all the questions. The more the breeder asks, the more she is seriously considering you as a candidate for one of her wonderful puppies.

Choosing a Puppy

Many puppy buyers expect to visit the breeder and select their favorite from a litter of several puppies. In reality, getting a good-quality puppy does not often work that way for several reasons. Litter sizes for toy breeds are relatively small, four to five puppies on average. One or more of them might be reserved either for the breeder or for people looking for a show dog. If you are looking for only a male or only a female, the choices will be limited by what is available in the litter. Many breeders feel that they know the puppies so well that they can better recommend the puppy best suited for you. If you have been selected to get a puppy from a reputable breeder, even if you do not get to pick it, you can consider the puppy chosen just for you.

BRINGING YOUR HAVANESE HOME

You are almost there. You have found a breeder; the litter has been born; and you are going to get a Havanese puppy. Now what? It is time to go shopping. Your new family member will need and enjoy many things.

What to Get Before Your Havanese Arrives

A dog has to eat, so a food bowl is needed. A pint-sized stainless steel bowl is suitable. It is unbreakable, unchewable, and easy to clean. A nontip bowl will keep the food from being scattered all over, either by accident or by mischieviousness. You may use a stainless steel water bowl of the same size. A water bottle, such as those used by rabbits, where the puppy licks water from a tube at the bottom, helps the puppy's coat on his muzzle stay dry.

After eating, a nap is in order. You can choose from many beds for your Havanese. There are mats and pads of varying thicknesses, fabrics,

Inviting a Havanese to join your family and your life is a big decision; resolve to be the best and most responsible dog owner that you can be.

stuffings, and styles. There are bolster or donut beds, beanbags and pillows, and expensive designer beds. Your dog does not need just one. Whatever you select, get one that is easily cleaned. Include a mat that will fit into her crate.

A crate: Seriously consider having a crate. It is a private place your dog can retreat to, and it greatly improves the task of housebreaking. It makes traveling easier. Wire crates are very durable and allow the puppy to see out. Crates are not jails or punishment. They should be delightful refuges with soft cushy beds, lots of toys, and chewies. The crate door can be kept open when your Havanese is not confined so she can go in and out at will.

Gates: Your new addition should not have full run of the house initially, at least until she is trained and reliably housebroken. The crate alone is too small for her primary area. Her place should still be in the midst of wherever the family spends the most time. Baby gates are very

Your Havanese is playful and energetic and loves toys that move and make sounds.

useful for keeping your dog from off-limits areas or inside some rooms. Select barriers with openings small enough that a Havanese cannot sneak through or get a head or leg caught in a gap.

A pen: If you want to confine your puppy to a part of a room, playpens or exercise pens (ex-pens) are excellent. With a playpen, make sure the sides will not allow escape. An ex-pen is a portable fence with hinged panels that can be used to corral your Havanese in or away from off-limits areas. You can use a couple of the ex-pens together to make a larger area for the dog. If your area is carpeted, put something on the carpet under the ex-pen to protect it until your puppy is reliably housebroken. A remnant of vinyl, plastic, plastic-coated fabric, or a tarp larger than the area enclosed by the ex-pen will work.

Collars and leads: Your puppy's collar should be lightweight and soft. A quick-clip nylon collar allows adjustment for size. Some owners like rolled leather. Although you should be able to slip a finger or two under it easily, it must be sized so that when you take her for a walk, she absolutely, positively cannot slip out of the collar. Check your growing puppy's collar weekly so that you can enlarge or replace it when it gets too small. Harnesses are often recommended for toy dogs. Both harnesses and collars may cause mats where they rub the hair; a harness covers a larger area so it could produce more mats.

Because of the matting, many owners do not leave the collar on their dog in the house. Others feel that a collar with a lightweight tag with the dog's name and owner's phone number is insurance if the dog runs off. You do not

---

TIP

"Homemade" Toys

Give your Havanese "made up" toys: a carrot, an orange, an ice cube, an empty box, or a plastic bottle that bounces in odd directions. Dogs, like children, get tired of old toys and love new ones, so be imaginative and creative. Do not give your puppy something you would not otherwise want her to play with; she does not know the difference between old shoes and socks and new ones.

want lots of heavy tags hung on the collar on this diminutive dog, though. A microchip can also identify your dog, but special microchip devices are needed to read it.

With the collar, you will also need a lead. A lightweight 6-foot (2-m) nylon lead works well. Flexible leads that extend and then automatically retract back into a handheld case are popular. This style gives the puppy a longer lead and avoids her getting tangled in excess lead lying on the ground.

Toys!

All children love toys, and your Havanese is a quintessential child. Objects that squeak, squeal, and move will enthrall your perennial puppy. Make sure that nothing on the toy (eyes, buttons, or such) is small enough to chew off and swallow. Insure that the toy itself is not small enough to swallow or gag on. Include toys meant for chewing, supervising so that she does not chew off a piece that could be choked on. Chew toys provide alternatives to items you do not want your puppy to chew, like furniture, shoes, and most everything else in your home.

"Toilet"ries: With a small dog, you have housebreaking choices. Every dog should learn to relieve herself outside; but there are other choices as well. You will want to determine your plans before your Havanese arrives and shop for what you need. You might want to continue what your breeder has been using for the puppy.

A toy dog can be trained to use a doggy litter box that uses special doggy litter. Many owners use piddle pads, absorbent pads similar to disposable diapers. Secure the pads, perhaps in a frame for that purpose, lest the puppy shred the pad. A doggy door allows your

An exercise pen can confine your puppy while giving her more room to play.

Havanese to go in and out as needed.

Male dogs in general are harder to housebreak than females. Many owners use belly bands on their boys. Put this onto your shopping list if you are getting a boy and want to use one.

You will be grooming your Havanese from the time you bring her home. Ask her breeder which products he uses and recommends to you. The chapter "Good Grooming" discusses products and tools you may want to get.

Make an appointment with your veterinarian for a day or two after your puppy will arrive. This visit will be to verify that the puppy is as healthy as the breeder represented and to review the vaccination schedule. Insert a microchip if the breeder has not already done so. A microchip, the size of a grain of rice, is inserted between a dog's shoulder blades by

Toys are more than just fun. They stimulate the senses, exercise muscles, provide acceptable chewing opportunities, and distract your puppy from playing with your toys.

your veterinarian and should be recorded in a national microchip registry to allow your dog to be identified and returned to you should she ever escape or get lost.

Find out from your breeder what your puppy has been eating so that you can continue the same food, amount, and schedule. Purchase some of that food just before she will arrive.

Puppy Proofing Your Home

Decide what room(s) or portions of room(s) your Havanese will have access to initially. For a young puppy, a more limited access will help you to avoid problems. The area/room should be one where most of the family spends most of the time. Ideally it will also be a place where you can quickly and frequently get her outside to potty. Baby gates, ex-pens, crates, and playpens are excellent tools to limit your

puppy's area while she is learning the house rules and are invaluable in housebreaking.

After selecting her places, get down onto the floor and look at the world from your

A Towel from Home

Whenever possible, get a towel or something similar that has been in the breeder's puppy area and that smells like the mother and puppies. This will comfort your puppy on her trip home and during her initial adjustment. She does not know why she is leaving all that she has ever known; the towel will smell like her first home and will ease the transition.

Havanese's perspective. Remember that puppies explore the world with their mouths. In your puppy's area, pick up or put out of the way anything that could hurt her. Look for pins, string, paper clips, paper, and cigarettes. Cords, plugs, and electric outlets can be lethal to puppies. Make sure that cleaning products, sponges, and medicines are behind closed doors. Snacks that you might enjoy—chocolate, grapes, and raisins—are toxic to dogs. If she goes with you to the garage, insure that she cannot get to antifreeze, paint products, pesticides, or anything else that is poisonous. Do not ever leave her in the garage, by the way; your Havanese is 100 percent a house dog.

While you are protecting her from things, also protect her from potentially dangerous places. Balconies, stairwells, patios with big drops to the ground, and open banisters can be perilous for your puppy. She should never have access to a swimming pool unless you are with her. Banister guards and pool guards as well as baby gates and ex-pens can be used as barriers.

Some plants and plant products are very toxic to dogs, and small dogs are much more seriously affected. Read labels to see if products can be used around pets. In the yard, check that your Havanese cannot wiggle under a fence. Your intelligent dog may well figure out how to open standard gate latches, so be prepared to lock them if you have an escape artist.

What to Get with Your Puppy

When you get your puppy, you should also get several things from your breeder. Discuss these ahead of time so that you both have the same expectations.

Your breeder should provide a sales agreement or contract for your puppy. Review this in detail ahead of time to make sure you agree with the terms. The agreement should include the AKC litter number, the full names and AKC numbers of both the dam and sire, and guarantees. Many list the conditions under which the

Dog food dishes come in many styles and materials.

TIP

Havanese Weights

Newborn Havanese weigh about 6 to 8 ounces (170 to 227 g). At eight weeks, she has grown to 3 to 4 pounds (1.4 to 1.8 kg) and 4 to 6 pounds (1.8 to 2.7 kg) by 12 weeks. At six months, depending on the height of the Havanese, her weight can range from 6 to 12 pounds (2.7 to 5.4 kg).

dog will be housed. It should state that the breeder will take back the dog if necessary.

AKC registration papers should be provided with the puppy. The only exception to this is if the breeder holds them until you spay or neuter your Havanese. If this applies to you, make sure you see either the AKC registration form or the AKC litter registration form (not an application)

Keep your puppy away from toxic plants inside and out.

to get the litter number and AKC registration numbers of the sire and dam.

You should also get a health record for your puppy. Take this document to your first veterinarian appointment. Get copies of any health certifications your puppy has had.

Your breeder will provide a pedigree for your Havanese, which is a record of the dogs in her ancestry usually to four generations. The dogs in the pedigree are registered with AKC as purebred Havanese. Dogs from other countries are registered with those countries' equivalent registries.

Learn from your breeder what training the breeder has done so far, which should include some housebreaking and socialization. If he has microchipped the puppy, get the microchip number and the registry it is listed with.

Traveling Home

If your breeder lives close enough, you can drive your Havanese home. A crate can comfortably confine the puppy for the trip. If you do not have a crate, have two people in the car: one to drive and the other to hold the puppy. If the trip is longer than an hour, plan potty stops. Make sure you have a collar that fits and leash to use if you have to stop to walk her to relieve herself.

Avoid problems by not letting the puppy eat or drink within two hours of the trip. Do not sedate her; drugs will make her disoriented and confused. If the trip will take several hours, freeze some water in a container to put into her crate. She can lick it periodically to get a drink, and it will not spill. Provide some toys and chew toys in the crate plus the towel that smells like Mom and home.

If your breeder lives too far away to drive to, consider an airplane. Few breeders will ship a young puppy, although some will ship an adult. If you do ship, your Havanese will need an airline-approved crate. Consider the time of day and geography to select the most comfortable travel weather. There is a temperature range in which the airlines will agree to ship a dog. Although they do allow an animal to travel in warmer or cooler temperatures with veterinarian approval, do not do it; it is too risky and uncomfortable for the dog.

Earlier flights and those that originate at the departure airport are less likely to be delayed or have mechanical problems. If possible, use nonstop flights, even if you have to drive to another airport. The airline will tell you their requirements for flying a dog.

You Are Home!

Schedule your puppy's arrival during a calm time at your house. Ideally someone should be home full-time with the puppy as she gets settled. Do not overwhelm your puppy. Let her make the advances and decide what she is ready for. Remember that she is a baby and does not know what is happening.

When your new puppy arrives home, take her to the place you want her to use to relieve herself. If she has been crated, she will be ready to go. Let her investigate her new area. When she goes, tell her what a good girl she is in a calm, friendly voice.

Show her where she can have a drink of water. Introduce her to the inside area that will be hers. Let her explore if she is inclined to do so. Have family members sit down or get down on the floor to meet her. Young children can hold the puppy on their laps only when sitting on the floor.

▬ CHECKLIST ▬

Places to Go with Your Havanese
- ✔ Veterinarian
- ✔ Parks (if allowed)
- ✔ Your or other places of business (if allowed)
- ✔ Neighborhood walks
- ✔ Pet superstore
- ✔ Groomer
- ✔ Neighbors' homes and yards
- ✔ Family members' homes and yards
- ✔ In front of stores in strip malls
- ✔ Picnics
- ✔ Puppy kindergarten classes
- ✔ Obedience classes
- ✔ Agility classes
- ✔ Kennels
- ✔ Dog shows
- ✔ Dog beaches
- ✔ Assisted-living and nursing homes
- ✔ Car trips
- ✔ Plane trips
- ✔ Playgrounds (if allowed)
- ✔ Little League games and other sporting events
- ✔ Vacations
- ✔ Wherever well-behaved dogs are allowed

Lifting and holding: Be careful when lifting her; only adults and older children should be allowed to do so. To pick her up, put a hand under her chest, with two fingers between her front legs, and put the other hand under her rump; hold her close to your body. Make sure

A towel that smells like her original home will ease the transition to her new home.

A crate a Havanese can travel in can become a bed at home.

she is held securely so she cannot wiggle out of your grasp and fall.

Above all, do not overwhelm her. Let her investigate her new surroundings and find her own comfort level. This is a big day for her—the biggest in her life so far. Make sure, especially with children, that she is not handled or played with roughly. She is a toy dog, not a stuffed toy.

Her own bed: Show her where her bed is, ideally in a crate that will function as her home within your home. Include in the crate a comfortable mat, toys, and chewies. She will appreciate the towel you brought from her breeder to make it smell more like home. Do not wash this towel unless absolutely necessary; the smells on it are comforting to your puppy. Place the crate within her area, somewhat out of the way, but where she can still see what is happening. If possible, place the crate near the door she will use to go outside to potty. With a small crate, you can conveniently have multiple units; you can also easily move a single crate around your home.

Give her undisturbed time in her crate to rest. If she fusses in her crate, take her to the place you want her to potty. After she has relieved herself, if she still fusses in her crate, you may attend to her to comfort her, or you may ignore her. If you go to her after she has become accustomed to your home, she is training you to come when called.

Since she is small, she will need to be taken out frequently; every hour or so is a good interval for a baby puppy. She may not sleep through the night until she is about three months old or more and accustomed to her new home.

Introducing the Rest of the Family

Let your Havanese meet the people in your home the day she arrives. If there are other animals in the household, have her meet each individually under close supervision. Other friendly dogs, especially big ones, may be too enthusiastic. Do not let them overpower her. Be careful when introducing her to other dogs, and watch both dogs' behavior and body language carefully for hints of aggression or reservation. Proceed slowly; better safe than sorry.

Most cats should not pose a risk to your puppy, but again watch their behavior. Cats often do not welcome new pets. Small pet birds also should be no problem. Do not leave her with large pet snakes that might be a danger to a small animal, including a small dog.

For introductions, consider putting the puppy into her crate and letting her and another pet sniff each other through the crate door. You can progress to their greeting through a baby gate

A lightweight lead and well-fitting collar come in many stylish colors

or ex-pen. You can then hold your Havanese while they continue to get acquainted. Make sure they behave well together in the house before letting them in the yard together. Some dogs may never share the same yard safely, so take each step slowly.

Socialization

One of your puppy's first trips outside her new home is to the veterinarian for the appointment you made before she arrived. Within a day or two of her arrival, you can begin short walks in the neighborhood that provide exercise, lead training, and introductions to your neighbors. If friendly dogs are in the neighborhood, she can meet them, too, under supervision.

The more friendly people, including men, women, and children, that your Havanese can meet, the better. The more nice places and gentle dogs she can visit, the better. Including

Beds come in many styles and materials. Make sure those you get can be easily cleaned.

Your imagination is the only limit about where you can take your Havanese. How about a beach where dogs are allowed?

these in your puppy's life is what socialization is all about. You cannot overdo providing new, positive experiences in her first several months of life. It is up to you to guarantee beyond a shadow of a doubt beforehand that they will be positive experiences.

The goal of socialization is to produce a happy, self-confident, well-adjusted adult who finds the world a friendly place. Socialization is a lifelong process. It does not stop when your dog gets to be six months or a year old. From the beginning, include your Havanese in your life and activities whenever you can.

Puppy Grooming

A goal of puppy grooming is to acclimate both you and your puppy to daily or every other day grooming. They will be short sessions, 5 or 10 minutes in length. She has a short puppy coat and a short puppy attention span. Grooming should be mutually enjoyable, part of your quality time together.

Include nail trimming in your puppy grooming sessions.

A harness may be used instead of a collar. The lead clips to a ring on the harness, and off you go.

The daily grooming for a Havanese revolves around brushing and coat care. You need a small grooming table with a nonskid surface. Get one with adjustable legs, because you will be sitting at it while you groom and need to modify it to the height of your chair, stool, or sofa. You need a soft pin brush, a steel comb, and a spray bottle of water to which some conditioner has been added.

Have your Havanese on the grooming table lying on her side. Hold her there with one hand on her shoulders until she is accustomed to the process. Mist the section of hair you are working on. Brush the hair section, making sure there are absolutely no tangles or mats. When an area is brushed through, you can comb through it as well. She does not have much hair as a puppy, but you two can practice the process together.

Every Havanese deserves a crate that is her home within a home. The door can be left open or closed as needed.

This is not playtime or punishment time. Although it should be pleasant and relaxing, the focus is on the grooming. For a more complete discussion of grooming your Havanese, see the chapter "Good Grooming."

LIVING WITH A HAVANESE

You selected a Havanese because you wanted a smart, small, friendly dog with a nonshedding coat that is good with children and other pets. Your life will be delightfully changed when you include this dog as a member of your family.

Considerations with a Toy Dog

Toy dogs were developed over the centuries to be companions. They were bred down from larger dogs. Toy dogs were used as lap and foot warmers before central heating. They were also used to attract fleas away from their humans long ago, before hygiene and pest control became as effective as they are today. However, their primary function has always been to provide love and friendship.

Behavior: Allowing a Havanese to misbehave is easy because he is small and cute, but this does him a disservice. He needs guidance and training to mold his personality and behavior to become a pleasant member of your family.

Make sure your Havanese cannot get into anything he cannot get out of.

Many dogs can become little tyrants if they make the house rules instead of the owners making them. (See the chapter on "Training and Recreation.")

Food: A Havanese eats less than a larger pet, so you can provide premium-quality food for him without straining your budget. It is also easier to unbalance his diet by giving him too many treats or leftovers. His growth and development, health and well-being depend on the food he eats. You can include crunchy food in his diet for his chewing enjoyment while helping to keep his teeth clean.

Size: A Havanese offers many advantages just by being small, up to 11½ inches (29.2 cm) tall and 12 pounds (5.4 kg). He will live longer, about 14 to 15 years on average, than larger breeds. He easily fits into almost any size home, from an apartment to an estate. He is easy to take with you wherever you travel, by car or by airplane.

Although he is small, your Havanese is a sturdy, rugged little dog, not frail or fragile. He should be allowed to walk on lead wherever it is safe and permitted rather than carried or confined to a carrier. He is willing and eager to participate in whatever the family does. Although he needs smaller amounts of many

Make sure your Havanese is always safe outside.

supplies and equipment, this does not apply to his purchase price. Havanese are not inexpensive. The starting price for a pet-quality dog is about $1,800, and prices are much higher for a show-quality animal.

Safety First

Because of his size, you must be alert to conditions and situations that could be dangerous to your Havanese. A small dog moving quickly can easily trip a person who does not notice him. Accidentally stepping on a Havanese paw can cause serious damage. Watch your step to avoid tripping or injuring your pet if he dances at your feet or sleeps in your path. Watch, too, when closing doors so that the door does not close on your pet.

He can get under and behind objects and into spaces you thought were too small for a dog and hide or be unable to get out. Garages, especially, may have nooks and crannies that a dog can investigate. If doors are opened when you do not know where he is, your Havanese can escape outdoors to the dangers located there. Even though he is devoted to you, he can run amazingly fast and be gone in a flash.

Poisons: Be very careful with pesticides and insecticides inside and out. Neurological damage or even death can result from these poisons. Cleaning products, medicines, and other toxic substances must be kept safely behind closed doors that your dog cannot open. Some plants are poisonous to dogs; others can produce allergic reactions. Even chocolate, an essential of life to many of us, is poisonous to a dog, so store it out of Havanese reach. A quantity of a toxic substance that might make a bigger dog sick can kill your petite canine.

Swimming pool safety: Some Havanese like to swim. If you have a pool, ensure that your dog cannot accidentally fall in. If you let him swim, make sure that someone is with him to supervise and to help him get out when he is ready. Practice with him so he can find the steps out. Hanging a tennis ball over the steps gives him a way to locate the exit. Havanese have been trapped beneath pool covers, so do not consider a pool cover as protection against your dog falling into the pool.

Chlorine and other chemicals used in swimming pools may discolor your dog's coat or irritate his skin or eyes. If you allow him to swim, rinse him thoroughly afterward with fresh, clean water. If you keep his coat long, he will be harder to rinse and dry, and you might find a swim more trouble than it is worth.

Good fences: An exercise pen, or ex-pen, is useful in limiting your dog's access either inside or outside. Some barriers that are effective with children and larger dogs may not contain a Havanese. The barriers should have openings small enough that your puppy cannot wiggle through or catch his head or paw in them.

A fenced yard must be examined to make certain your Havanese cannot escape. Small gaps between the lower edge of the fence and the ground can be avenues to unfortunate adventures. You can run 18-inch-tall (45-cm) poultry wire with 1-inch (2.5-cm) holes along the ground and wrapped up onto the fence to close those gaps. End posts may not be set close enough to the house, wall, or another fence, leaving a small space that must be closed off with an extra board.

Your Havanese is very intelligent; the more he learns, the more he can learn.

TIP

Birds of Prey Dangerous to Small Dogs
- ✔ Eagles
- ✔ Falcons
- ✔ Hawks
- ✔ Ospreys
- ✔ Owls

Your Havanese will enjoy surveying the world perched on the back of the couch.

Unfriendly neighbors: Wild animals prey on small dogs. In some parts of the United States, coyotes have stolen dogs out of yards. Even with a secure fence, large birds such as hawks and eagles can swoop down and take a small dog. Snake bites can kill pets. If wildlife dangers exist near your home, accompany your Havanese on trips to the yard. Some owners limit their dogs to screened-in or covered lanais or patios for exercise.

Furniture: Many owners invite their Havanese up onto the furniture. Pick him up properly by putting one hand under his chest, behind his front legs, and the other hand supporting his rear. All the family should use the proper procedure. Do not allow small children to pick up or carry him if there is any chance they might drop him. They can hold and pet the Havanese on their laps when they are sitting down. When he is on the furniture, do not let your dog jump down from any height he could not jump up on to.

A People-Loving Temperament

The primary function of a Havanese is to be a delightful companion to his family. This breed is very friendly and affectionate, always wanting to be near you and eager for petting and kisses. Gentle and responsive to what his people want, this dog is very sensitive to your voice, your actions, and your behavior. A Havanese is sociable and needs to be with his family, so this breed does not do well if you do not have the time to spend with him. He needs and thrives on human companionship, loving to cuddle and be close to you.

Your Havanese is a playful clown who enjoys games and invents mischief to keep himself busy. Although this may not appeal to everyone, his clever and comical nature is part of his charm. The more you play with him, the more delighted and bonded you two will be. His antics are a continual source of entertainment for you and your family.

Intelligence: The fun-loving nature of a Havanese is accompanied by a high level of intelligence. They are easy to train in obedience and quickly learn to perform tricks. They may well be the stars in their obedience class. They have been successfully used as circus dogs due to their cleverness and pleasure in working for and with their people. Because of their responsiveness to people, they are very sensitive to the tone of your voice. Harsh words and tones of voice will upset your Havanese and are not effective. This breed really shines with positive reinforcement.

Watchdogs: Because of their alertness, Havanese are good watchdogs. They will bark to let you know you have company. They are much too friendly and too small to offer any protection. They will welcome your guests, not guard against them.

Some Havanese bark more than others. You can teach the more talkative individuals not to bark. This is best done when they are young and before barking becomes a habit. One method is to put your fingers around your Havanese's muzzle and say "Quiet" or "Hush" whenever he barks. As soon as he stops, release his muzzle and praise him. Soon, you can say "Hush," and your puppy will be quiet.

Preferences: Velcro dog—that is how people refer to Havanese. They want to be with you,

wherever you go. When you are on the computer, they will be next to you. When you watch television, they will cuddle with you on the couch. When you make a trip to the bathroom, well, they want to accompany you everywhere.

Havanese like to be up high so they can see what is happening. They especially like the tops of upholstered chairs or the sofa. Your dog may climb onto the back of the couch, rest his head on your shoulder, and then fall asleep. They prefer being on the furniture to the floor and consider it more special to share the furniture with their special person. If you have multiple Havanese, you might find one on each shoulder.

Space and Exercise Needs

Havanese do not need much space and do very well in apartments or condominiums as well as in houses with yards. Their primary requirement is that they are with their people rather than confined to a kennel, patio, or yard.

Their exercise needs are moderate to high, about average for dogs of their size. They will enjoy a few walks a day if you can accommodate them. Your Havanese will be taking many more steps during the walk than you do, so notice if he is getting tired and needs to return home.

Outside: Most Havanese owners allow their dogs to enjoy their yards, accompanying them if there is any danger from wildlife. Remove dirt, brush, leaves, and twigs from the yard; these can tangle in your dog's coat. Even after you have tidied, trees can drop seeds and leaves to be picked up in the coat. Coat care will be easier if you examine your dog's coat whenever he comes in from outside so that you can comb the hair, remove any collected debris, and dry damp hair before mats are formed.

Enclosures: Some owners restrict their Havanese to a screened, covered, or enclosed lanai for exercise and bathroom duties. The surface, instead of grass, is usually concrete, tile, or some other surface that is easier on the dog's coat. Such places can offer a larger area for playtime while being more protective of the dog and his coat.

Inside the home, Havanese may sometimes be busy and active but are generally relatively quiet. The more exercise they get outside, the less rowdy they will be in the house.

Even so, once in awhile, your Havanese will get the "zoomies" and turn your home into a racetrack. After flying off the back of the couch, he will zoom through the living room, dash into the dining room, circle around the kitchen, and race around and around. He may bank off the furniture, skid on tile, and leap over obstacles. His eyes will shine with glee, a

Have children sit on the floor to hold your Havanese.

smile on his face, his tongue hanging out, and his hair blowing in the wind. The race may last for several minutes before he flops in cheerful exhaustion, happily spent, until next time.

Havanese and Children

The basic nature of a Havanese plus their sturdy construction makes them excellent companions for most children. That said, there are two things to be discussed. First, Havanese are dogs. Second, children need to treat dogs—all dogs—properly.

Teaching the Havanese About Children

You may have heard that the Havanese is the perfect breed for children. Compared with other breeds that are less tolerant of children and given the typical temperament of Havanese, this is generally true. However, this good relationship does not magically happen. All puppies, including Havanese, have needle-sharp teeth. Initially, they will put their teeth on everything, including people. This is how they interacted with their mothers and littermates. They need to be trained not to put their mouths on people, including children, to learn not to treat children as they would their littermates. They are not born knowing how to deal with children; you must teach them. See the chapter "Training and Recreation" on how to control nipping.

Adult Havanese also have teeth. If a dog is completely unaccustomed to children and feels abused or threatened, he will struggle, growl, and try to get away from his tormentor. If all else fails, he may bite. Since biting is unacceptable, it is incumbent on the adults involved, the owners of the dog and parents of the child, to

Supervise the playtime of children and your Havanese to ensure that it is a totally successful experience for both.

make sure biting never happens and never to put the dog in that situation.

Socialize your Havanese, as a puppy if possible, with well-behaved children so that he knows what fun it can be to play with them and get all the attention. If he is an adult and has not been around children or is not comfortable with them, let him meet one child at a time. Have the child be quiet and not very active. Let the child sit and pet the dog; let the child walk him slowly on a lead. Have the child give him a special treat. The Havanese will enjoy the gentle attention.

Teaching Children About the Havanese

Children, too, must be taught how to behave around puppies and dogs. They must respect the dog and not do anything to the dog that they would not want done to themselves by complete strangers. No pulling legs, ears, coat, or tail.

TIP

Critical Socialization Period

Even though socialization is a lifelong process, the time between 8 and 16 weeks is especially critical. The more positive, happy, pleasant experiences you can include in this time period, the bigger the positive influence these experiences will have on your dog's personality and temperament.

No poking the dog in the eyes or any place else. Never drop him, fall on him, or step on him.

Children must learn not to overwhelm the puppy or be rowdy around him. Teach the children to be calm and pet the dog, to talk to him softly and gently, and not to scream or yell. Do not let them lean over the dog, especially if he is sleeping. Do not let them bother him when he is eating. Do not let them hug or squeeze the dog. Dogs show affection with physical contact, but not by hugging. Dogs endure hugging from people, but they would prefer some other form of affection. If you doubt it, look at a person hugging a dog. The person looks happy, but the dog does not.

Never let a small child play with a Havanese puppy unsupervised. This is not necessarily the right breed for toddlers who have not learned how to handle a dog gently. No child should be allowed to carry a Havanese if there is any possibility the dog might be dropped.

Your Havanese should be comfortable wherever he goes, whether or not he brings his own chair.

Havanese are kids themselves. They are natural playmates for children provided the puppy or dog has learned how to play with children and, just as important, the children have learned how to treat a little dog. If they treat each other well, they can entertain each other for hours.

Havanese and Other Pets

This cheerful breed is very friendly, and this friendliness extends to other animals in your household. They enjoy the company of other dogs, especially other Havanese. That said, some dogs might not be the best companions for your puppy.

Large dogs that were bred to chase down and kill small, running animals such as rabbits might not do well with any small dog when both are running loose in a large yard. A running Havanese might trigger a primitive instinct with very unfortunate results. Be very careful before letting a Havanese loose to run in a large area with a dog that has a strong prey drive. Once they develop a strong friendship, they should be safe together.

Some individual dogs are dog aggressive. These can be a real danger to your Havanese. If you have a larger dog that is dog aggressive, be very slow and careful in introducing your Havanese.

This does not mean that Havanese do not do well with most dogs, including large dogs. One owner tells of her Havanese going into her Doberman's crate, curling up, and sleeping in the crook of the bigger dog's elbow.

Cats, not historically best friends with dogs, can be great pals with Havanese. The social nature of the Havanese replaces any canine prey drive that might threaten the cat. An owner tells of her Persian cat and Havanese playing and sleeping together, jumping and chasing each other like any two playmates.

Socialization

Most Havanese are extroverts due to the breed and individual temperament; but they are also influenced by their experiences, especially as puppies. You can make a positive difference by socializing your puppy.

The purpose of socializing is to produce a happy, well-adjusted, confident dog that finds the world a friendly place. For a young puppy, almost everything is new. When he is most receptive, as a puppy, is a good time to expose him to as many new people, places, animals, and things as you can. The more positive experiences he has as a youngster, the more comfortable he will be with new experiences for the rest of his life. You must prescreen his new experiences to make sure they reinforce the view that the world is a friendly, welcoming, and happy place.

Neighbors and friends: When you have people come to your house, if they are agreeable, have them meet your Havanese. He will be in your guest's lap given the slightest opportunity. Take him for walks in the neighborhood, always on lead, and introduce him to your neighbors and their children. Go for walks in area parks. Take him anywhere you can where dogs are welcome.

Many obedience clubs and some pet supply stores offer puppy kindergarten classes that are excellent places for your Havanese to meet other people and other dogs in a new location. Gentle introductory training is offered, but the real value is the new experiences it offers your puppy.

Apprehension: As your Havanese encounters new people, animals, and places, if he meets them confidently, encourage him and praise him. If he is nervous or anxious, do not coo, soothe, or pet him, as that will reinforce his apprehension. Instead, act confidently—you are his leader. He will look to you for an appropriate attitude. Do not push him; let him approach at his own speed. As he meets more new people, animals, and places and nothing bad happens, and as he sees you confident and unafraid, he will become more confident, too.

If he is food motivated, carry some extra-special treats with you. When he meets a new

This Havanese assumes he's invited to the picnic.

Havanese enjoy the company of other pets, whether they are other Havanese or other breeds.

person, if she is willing, slip her a couple of treats to feed your Havanese. He will learn that new people are wonderful and a source of goodies.

When You Travel

When you go on a trip and stay at a place that allows dogs, take him. However, you may occasionally need to take trips without your dog. If you think you might use a pet sitter in the future, arrange for a friend whom your Havanese knows to come to your home when you are not there, let him out in the yard, and feed him. You can inquire whether his breeder, if she lives nearby, can keep him when you are gone. Nearby friends or relatives are good pet sitters, in your home or theirs. If this option is available, you can have him visit their homes ahead of time to get to know them.

Kennels: If your only option is a kennel, do your research and preparation ahead of time. If your dog's first experience being kenneled is when he is older, he may be stressed, even refusing food or getting sick. To avoid the stress, give him the experience when he is young. Find an area kennel that is suitable for toy dogs, and let him stay there for the day or overnight a few times. Make sure the kennel is sized for and equipped to handle a toy dog. Many kennels separate large and small dogs. He needs to have an individual run and not be crated. Make sure it is a positive experience, with toys and treats, so that he has a good time and learns that you will come get him shortly.

When You Work

Havanese are very social dogs with strong needs to be with their family and have much interpersonal interaction. Their primary desire is to be with you. If your Havanese had her choice, she would have you home all day.

Various options: This is not always possible; some people have to work to buy dog food. You can consider some options to accommodate your pet. Some lucky owners can take their dog to work. Others can come home for lunch and dog attention and affection. Nearby family, a neighbor, or a pet sitter can stop by, let the dog out, and provide play and petting. Doggy day care establishments are proliferating and offer a busy social day for your dog, including some training as well.

An adult Havanese should not be confined to a small crate for a whole day nor can he be kept outside during the day. This is not an outside breed, if any is. If you leave him alone, you should provide a larger area for the dog, perhaps a small room, portion of a room, or an exercise pen.

Another dog? A good solution for a very sociable dog if you need to work full-time is to have another family member keep him company: another dog member of the family. Havanese want to be with their family, which includes their extended family, which includes the family pets.

Another dog to keep your Havanese company will relieve his loneliness. A cat, too, can provide companionship. They can entertain each other, keep each other company, and share secrets. While you are gone, they can plan mischief and new games. Often, with two dogs in a family, they will eat better, although they should be fed separately to avoid arguments or having one eat more than his share and get fat. What your Havanese would like best of all would be another Havanese.

It is better to get each dog separately and one at a time. Train, bond, and love the first dog first. Then get the second. Make sure when the second dog arrives that the first dog knows that he is still senior in your affections. Pet him first, feed him first, and give him treats first so he will not be jealous. Give him first access to your lap and his favorite position on the furniture. Most likely, he will eagerly welcome the new member of the family.

Getting a young pup as company for the aged dog is not always kind. The senior is not interested in romping with the pesky youngster, and the new fellow does not really have a buddy to play with. Although your two dogs do not have to be the same age, both will be happier if they are not too many years apart and have similar activity and energy levels.

Like potato chips, it is hard to have just one Havanese.

HAVANESE NUTRITION

You are what you eat, and so is your dog. Her dietary needs will vary with her age, activity level, and general health. You have the responsiblity of selecting an appropriate, high-quality food that will allow her to be all that she can be.

Puppy Diets

When your puppy first arrives, feed her the same food and amount and on the same schedule that the breeder used with the litter. This will ease the puppy's transition to your home and help avoid any tummy upsets that might occur during this stressful time. If you like the food, continue using it throughout her puppyhood. Increase the amount as she grows.

If you want to consider other foods, focus only on high-quality foods that are especially formulated for small or toy breed puppies. Your veterinarian and breeder can recommend the high-quality brands.

When looking at puppy foods for toy breeds, you should find that the pieces of food are fairly small, suitable for small mouths. They will have a higher calorie and protein level in an

A quality diet will produce a healthy, lustrous coat.

equivalent volume than foods for larger breeds. Small dogs cannot consume large amounts. However, they use lots of energy and need a food that is condensed into a smaller volume to fuel their activity.

Initially, feed your puppy three times per day. When she is about six months old or loses interest in the third meal, you can transition to feeding her twice a day. Many Havanese owners feed their dogs twice a day for the rest of their dogs' lives. With two meals, she does not have to be hungry for long periods and will have the energy for her busy day. Other owners feed just one meal daily, with snacks during the day. When she is about one year old, you can transition her to adult food.

Limit treats for toy breed puppies because their digestive system is delicate when they are young. Good food plus water should keep your Havanese healthier than a variety of different tidbits. Too many treats, especially human food, can cause soft stools. You can provide chew toys to aid with teething, but make sure your pup does not chew off a piece and swallow it.

How to Feed

Many styles of food bowls are available, but stainless steel bowls have many advantages. They are easy to clean, do not break, will not chip, and cannot be damaged by chewing. A 1-pint (475-mL) bowl is suitable for your Havanese. You can get a no-tip style if your puppy tends to knock it over.

Feed your Havanese at fixed times each day. You may also consider providing water at fixed times during housebreaking. Remember, what goes in on a schedule also comes out on a schedule.

Provide food and water for your dog in the same place each day so she will know where to expect it. Her crate makes an excellent place for her to eat in peace. If you have other animals, they cannot help themselves to her meal if fed in her crate. It also reinforces that the crate is a good place to be.

You can free-feed your Havanese: that is, leave the food down all the time so she can eat when she wants. This has some appeal in allowing the dog to decide when to eat, and you can just fill the bowl. It has some negatives, too. It makes housebreaking harder. You cannot take her out after eating, because you do not know when that is. She is likely to take a nugget of food somewhere else to eat it, perhaps on the couch or your bed, and you will find bits of food throughout the house. If you have multiple pets, you will not know how much each one is eating. Finally, the leader of the pack—you—should provide and control the food. With free feeding, your Havanese is in control.

When you feed your Havanese, preferably in her crate, leave her with the food for 20 minutes. Then pick up anything she has not eaten and refrigerate the leftover food. Use the leftovers as the basis of the next meal. Any food not eaten in two meals should be discarded.

A non-tip stainless bowl avoids spilled food and water.

Playing is good exercise and helps work up an appetite.

Toy Dog Food

Because Havanese do not eat large quantities of food, do not buy more dog food than you can use in a month. The vitamin potency fades in older dry dog food. The fats in dry food can become rancid.

Your Havanese will do best if you select a premium food that is formulated especially for toy and small breeds. Research has shown that small and toy dog metabolism is different from that of large and giant breeds. Toy dogs need to consume about double the number of calories for each pound of their body weight than larger dogs. Because Havanese have smaller stomachs, feeding two or even three times per day might be the best way to meet their needs.

Commercial Food

Commercial food comes in canned, semi-moist, and dry forms. Canned food has the most moisture (about 75 percent) and is often the most palatable. It is also the messiest and requires more cleaning of your Havanese's beard and mustache after eating. Semimoist food is not a good regular diet because of the high sugar content and the dyes used to make it look meaty; those dyes can actually affect your dog's coat color. Dry food or kibble is the most commonly used food and is the most healthy and economical. Although it is not as inherently tasty as the other forms, it has the benefit of helping to keep teeth clean when the dog crunches the nuggets.

A good brand: When selecting a food, stick to premium brands that have established reputations of consistent high quality. You are more assured of quality if the dog food is produced by a large company that has the funds to do adequate research, that has significant quality control, and that is carefully government

There are many food choices, and each dog is an individual. If your Havanese is doing well on a quality dog food, then there is no need to change.

inspected. Small company designer foods may lack effective quality controls and fly beneath government inspection radar. To insure the food is as fresh as possible, check the expiration date and shop at stores that turn over their inventory regularly.

Read labels: Ingredients are listed on the label in descending sequence by weight. The first or at least the second ingredient should be a meat product; preferably several of the first six items should be animal-based products. The label should name the specific meat, as in chicken, lamb, or fish rather than just "meat." With canned food, the first ingredient should be meat.

A chart on the label shows the percentages of protein, fat, moisture, and fiber in the food. Small-breed puppy foods should have a higher percent of protein and fat than other puppy foods. Small-breed adult foods should have a higher amount of protein and fat than dog food for larger dogs. This difference accommodates the Havanese's greater need for energy from the small amount of food she can eat.

With a high-quality, balanced food, you should not need to supplement your Havanese as a puppy or as an adult. In fact, supplementing with additives or other foods unbalances the diet and can actually cause health problems.

Treats

Dogs love treats. Treats are used for training, to reward good behavior, and just to be friendly. Be careful, though, in your selection of food for treats. You do not want to add fatty, salty, or nonnutritious foods as treats. Too many treats can unbalance your dog's diet, make her fat, or spoil her appetite. Even small dog biscuits can add up to a meal if given several times a day. If you break a small dog biscuit into multiple pieces, though, you have several treats to offer without feeding more than a couple of biscuits each day.

Many quality companies offer their dog and cat food in small sample bags. You can use the nuggets from the samples as treats. You might find a brand that your Havanese finds particularly tasty.

Homecooked Food

The primary challenge in cooking for your Havanese at home is getting the food balanced. Your veterinarian can recommend a recipe prepared by canine nutritionists for a small breed that will supply your dog's needs. Since getting precise balance with the homemade diet is more difficult, use a small-breed commercial puppy food until your Havanese is a year old. Save the more creative meals for when she is grown up and can better tolerate a less-precise balance.

Raw Food

There are many proponents of a raw diet, which includes raw meat and bones, for dogs. A big selling point is that it is the natural diet of dogs in the wild. In case you have not noticed, Havanese do not exist in the wild. They are products of over 100,000 years of domestication, during which dogs scavenged human leftovers.

Wolves get most of their carbohydrates from eating partly digested food in the stomachs of their prey. The digestive systems of wolves, and dogs, are not designed to get nutrients from whole raw carbohydrates, so those parts of the raw diets pass through the dogs mostly unused.

Raw meats may contain bacteria, including *Escherichia coli* and *Salmonella*, which can make your dog sick. Havanese do not have the jaws to chew raw bones thoroughly enough, and bone fragments can get stuck in their digestive tracts.

No controlled studies to date have confirmed that raw diets are balanced and safe for dogs in general. For all these reasons, raw diets are not a good choice for a small breed like a Havanese.

Water

Water is critical for your dog's health. A dog can go longer without food than without water. When your Havanese is a puppy, you may want to provide water only at regularly scheduled

When she looks longingly and you provide a treat, she is training you, which is fine if you are agreeable.

TIP

A Turkey by Any Other Name

If an ingredient is a part of the name of the food, such as Turkey and Barley Dog Food, those ingredients—turkey and barley—must together be 95 percent of the contents. Additionally, the first listed ingredient must be at least 50 percent of the total. However, words like *dinner* or *entree* in the product title means that the ingredients named may be a much lower percentage of the food. If the name says, "With chicken" or "chicken flavored," the food may contain 3 percent or less chicken. Be skeptical of fancy titles.

Various Chronic Illnesses and Suggested Diets

Condition	Diet Suggestions
Diabetes	High complex carbohydrates, no simple sugars, moderate protein, low fat; feed small, frequent meals
Liver disease	Protein source other than meat; include carbohydrates; minimum vitamin A and copper; feed small, frequent meals
Kidney disease	High-quality protein, such as beef or chicken; reduced phosphorous; minimum salt
Congestive heart failure	Minimum salt
Urinary stones	High-fiber vegetable diet low in calcium
Pancreatitis	Low fat

times until she is reliably housebroken. After that, always have clean, fresh water readily available.

Many owners use a water bottle with a tube at the bottom from which the dog can lick water. This arrangement keeps the facial hair dry. Your dog may not drink enough water with this device, however. If you suspect that yours is not, provide water in a bowl several times a day. After she finishes drinking, dry and comb her beard and mustache so she will not use your carpet and couch as a napkin.

TIP

Sources of Protein

Eggs and chicken are among the most easily digested protein by dogs. Beef and soy are harder for dogs to digest, and therefore dogs do not get as much benefit from these products.

Make sure your Havanese drinks only fresh, clean water and that the water bowl or bottle is cleaned regularly. Puppies can pick up *Coccidia* and *Giardia*, which infect the digestive tract, from stagnant water and then have severe diarrhea.

Picky Eaters

Many Havanese are picky eaters. They may not eat as well as they did at their breeder's home where they were competing with littermates for food. Things more interesting than food easily distract them. Feeding in a crate can limit the distractions, but Havanese are not usually hearty eaters.

As a result, some Havanese owners often add what they hope will be enhancements to the food to get their dogs to eat. You can add up to 10 percent without unbalancing your dog's diet. Some add a bit of cottage cheese, yogurt, or grated cheese. Watch for digestive upsets, though, for some dogs do not tolerate milk

When you travel, consider bringing water from home to avoid digestive upsets from drinking unfamiliar water.

Multiple dogs run together and exercise each other, which keeps them in good condition.

products well. You can add a small amount of finely cut meat, chicken, or fish. A spoonful of canned dog food or even cat food stirred into kibble can make it tastier. Some diced, cooked egg might appeal. A bit of baby food or warm broth might entice her to eat.

Trying to get a dog to eat is frustrating, offering one food enticement after another. Doing this actually teaches the dog to be picky—you are rewarding her disinterest in food by offering more and better tidbits. She may reject today the very food she liked yesterday.

One breeder suggests that dogs will eat with more gusto if they are less sure that the food

will appear on schedule. So once a week, all of his dogs miss a meal. Others reassure us that no healthy dog will starve herself to death. Remove the uneaten food if not eaten in 20 minutes. Your dog will be hungrier at the next meal. For this system to work, though, do not provide in-between-meal snacks and treats that will ruin her appetite. Hunger is a better sauce than anything you can add.

Do notice if loss of appetite is a symptom of possible illness. If your dog loses her normal appetite or her weight drops quickly, have her checked by your veterinarian. Your Havanese's reluctance to eat may be a health or dental problem. Your veterinarian visit should include a thorough exam of her mouth and teeth in addition to a general checkup.

The Too-Plump Pup

You are the lucky one! You have the one Havanese in 50 with a good appetite. Control of the situation is totally yours—well, yours and your family's; they must cooperate. Although obesity is not normally a problem in the breed, it can occur. Make sure that your girl has a waist, that you can feel her ribs, that she does not have a roll of fat at the bottom of her neck or base of her tail. Extra weight on a dog, just like on a person, can stress her organs and cause skeletal problems.

The solution is simply to reduce the amount of food she is getting. Before you start a diet, check with your veterinarian to make sure there is not a health component to the extra weight. Examine what your dog is eating. You might need to reduce the number of treats. If you want to retain the treats, reduce the amount you are feeding her at each meal. If she is able,

Dogs can develop allergies to foods and plants that previously didn't bother them at all.

increase her physical exercise playing in the yard or going for walks. The exercise will be good for you, too.

Special Diets

You are already tailoring your Havanese's food selections for her size and age. Other situations may dictate modified diets. Some specially formulated commercial diets are available from your veterinarian for certain conditions. Check with your veterinarian before you start a substantial diet change.

Geriatric dogs' digestive processes do not work as efficiently as younger dogs', so they need easily digestible foods. They are less active and can get overweight, which can exacerbate other health problems. You may choose a dog food formulated especially for seniors' needs. It should include sufficient high-quality protein. Seniors need more protein rather than less to keep their body in good repair since they may not get full value from the protein they eat. Foods containing antioxidants can help boost their immune system. Glucosamine and similar products can help maintain cartilage and joint strength.

Allergies: Dogs may develop allergies to many things, including fleas, dust, plants, and food. No current test can reliably identify the foods your Havanese might be allergic to. Hypoallergenic foods for your dog are available through your veterinarian.

Illness and diet: Some chronic illnesses are better managed with a modified diet. Consult with your veterinarian about the recommended diet.

GOOD GROOMING

A Havanese's coat is often the focus of grooming discussions. Remember to tend to ears, eyes, teeth, and nails, too.

Puppy Grooming

Your Havanese will be groomed frequently throughout his whole life, so acclimate him and yourself to the process shortly after he arrives. Plan short grooming sessions, five to ten minutes to start, every day or two.

Teach him to stand and to lie down for grooming. Initially, you may have to hold him with one hand, stroke him with the other hand, and talk to him until he relaxes. Be firm but kind; make it a pleasant time for him. Praise him when he is behaving well. You can end each session with a special treat as a reward.

During grooming, check for mats and attend to them immediately. If you do not, they will only get worse. Look for any sores, bumps, or

Good grooming shows.

parasites. Anything that causes your dog to scratch may end up producing mats.

Grooming Tools and Products

Consult your breeder for her recommendations about grooming tools. Ask what grooming she has done already with the puppies.

A grooming table will make grooming much easier for both of you. It should have a nonskid surface and be steady. A wobbly surface will make your dog nervous. He will not stand still, and he will dislike grooming. A table with adjustable legs lets you be comfortable working at it wherever you are sitting. Consider getting a grooming arm that will attach to the table and have a security loop worn by the dog to help keep him in place. Do not ever leave

Shampoo Can Burn

A tearless baby shampoo can be used to wash your Havanese's face. Other shampoos can sting his eyes. A tearless shampoo allows you to do a good job and still have the process comfortable for your dog.

the dog unattended on the table, though, for he can hang himself with the security loop or jump off and hurt himself.

Coat care equipment: A soft pin brush is the most useful for grooming a Havanese coat. A bristle brush can be more comfortable for a baby puppy. As the coat grows, though, the pin brush will work better. A slicker brush, with shorter tines, is useful for grooming feet. You will also need a metal comb. A flea comb is handy to remove the matter from the corners of the eyes. You might try several dog sham-

poos before you find the one that works best for your dog.

A dog coat conditioner used after his bath will make his coat easier to groom. A protein conditioner strengthens damaged hair. A spray bottle of water to which some conditioner has been added can be sprayed onto the coat when you brush your dog between baths. If you keep your Havanese's coat full length, consider investing in a blow-dryer especially made for use with dogs, which uses less-intense heat than the human version. Stands are available to target the hair dryer so you can brush while the coat is being blown dry.

Other grooming products: Special ear-cleaning products or witch hazel can be used with cotton balls and cotton swabs for ear cleaning. Tweezers are used to pull hair growing out of the dog's ears.

You will need a pair of scissors if you do any of your own trimming. Rounded or blunt-end scissors are safer to use. Do not use scissors on a dirty dog or you will dull them. An electric clipper is handy if you do your own grooming.

Bath Time

Even if you use a groomer for haircuts, you may want to bathe your Havanese yourself. Weekly baths will keep him clean and sweet smelling.

Brush and comb his coat thoroughly to remove all mats and tangles before wetting him. Put a cotton ball into each ear to keep out water. A drop of mineral oil in each eye helps protect from soap or water.

Grooming tools include styptic powder, nail clippers, pin brush, steel comb, scissors, and grooming table with grooming arm.

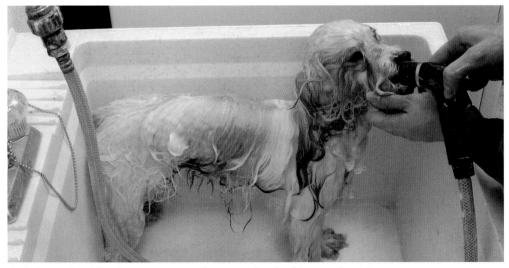

A sink or tub with a hose spray attachment makes bathing much easier.

You can bathe your dog in the kitchen sink, laundry tub, or bathtub. After wetting him thoroughly, work the shampoo into his coat, using only an amount to make good suds. Too much shampoo will make him harder to rinse. Remember to wash his face and ears, being careful to keep soap out of his eyes. A soft toothbrush can be used to clean around his eyes.

Rinse him thoroughly. Then rinse some more. A spray attachment on a hose lets you reach every crevice. Run your hands over him to see if any place feels even slightly soapy. You can easily miss his throat, chest and underside, armpits, and the inside of his thighs.

Wrap him in a thick bath towel to absorb as much water from his coat as you can. Put him onto the grooming table to dry and brush out his coat. Aim the blow-dryer at the part you are working on, brushing as the coat dries. Make sure you can brush and comb through the entire coat before you finish. Confirm that it is thoroughly dry as well.

Coat Care

Havanese hair grows similarly to the way human hair does. The Havanese coat can reach 6 to 8 inches (15 to 20 cm) in length. Some hairs fall out, as ours do, but Havanese do not shed their coat like other dogs do.

TIP

Stain Removal

A light-colored Havanese coat can benefit from the periodic use of a dog whitener product to remove stains. Spray it onto the stained area, wait, and then brush it out.

TIP

Cornstarch and Powder

Cornstarch or talcum powder can help dry and clean the damp and dirty parts of the coat. Sprinkle one into a wet coat to absorb the moisture, rub it in, and then brush it out with a pin brush. Comb through the coat to remove the excess. These can be used to clean his face or clean accidents at the other end. If the coat is not wet, mist it to dampen. These can be used to whiten a stained coat when brushing a newly bathed dog. Do not use on dark-colored coats.

Wrap your Havanese in a big towel after his bath to absorb the water and keep him from getting chilled.

The initial coat will be a puppy coat. At about a year of age, the adult coat starts to come in. The coat will mat more at this time. You must be especially dedicated to daily grooming and removing mats during the change. The transition lasts about two to three months.

Place your Havanese on his side on the grooming table to begin the coat-grooming session. Work with a section of coat at a time, making a horizontal part to separate the coat you are currently grooming and pushing the other out of the way. This is called *line brushing.* Each section should be about an inch (2.5 cm) wide. Do not go to the next section until the brush and comb go smoothly through the coat of the current section.

Unless your dog has just had a bath, mist the section of coat you are working on from the spray bottle containing the water and conditioner. Do not brush a dry coat, because the hair will break. Start at the back leg; brush the hair up and away from the body. You might use a bristle or slicker brush on the lower parts of the legs. Work sections up the leg to the hip, and then proceed to the front leg, again brushing the hair in sections. Section and work the coat on that side of the body.

When finished with the first side, turn the dog over to lie on his other side. Section, mist, and brush the coat on that side, again with the back leg first, followed by the front leg, and the body. Remember to brush both sides of each leg and the belly and chest when you are working the side of the body.

Stand the dog facing away from you. Section, mist, and brush the rear and tail. Protect the sensitive genital area from the brush with your hand. Comb through the coat to make sure no

With a dryer on a stand, both hands are free to hold and brush your Havanese.

fecal matter is in the hair. Continue up the back of the body.

Turn your dog around to groom the neck and chest. Remember to comb the armpits. Brush the ears inside and out. With the flea comb and cotton ball, remove any matter on the coat from the corner of the eye. Comb the face, beard, and mustache.

Some owners groom the coat in a different sequence. The order is your choice, so long as you do it often and thoroughly. Make brushing part of your quality time with your Havanese. Do it while watching television, listening to music, talking on the phone (with a headset). Just do it.

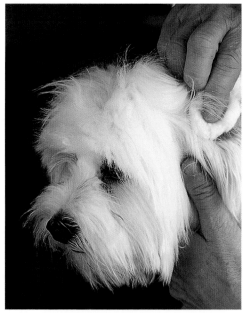

Regular ear cleaning helps avoid infections.

Weekly baths will keep your Havanese clean and sweet smelling. You can bathe your dog yourself in the kitchen sink or bathtub.

Caring for the Whole Dog

Caring for your Havanese involves more than taking care of just his coat. A responsible owner cares for the dog's ears, eyes, teeth, and nails. Proper and total care throughout the life of your Havanese can help prevent illnesses and other problems from occurring in the future.

Ear Care

A little ear cleaner or witch hazel on a cotton ball, just damp with the liquid squeezed out, is used to clean out the inside of your Havanese's ears. Use a cotton swab to wipe out crevices too small for cotton balls to reach. Excess hair growing in the ear canal should be pulled out to avoid infection. Sprinkle antibiotic powder in the ear first, and use tweezers to get a better grip. Folded ears like those of a Havanese are prone to ear infections, so keep his ears clean and dry.

Eye Care

Some Havanese eyes tear more than others. If you trim the hair at the corners of the eyes, you will need to keep trimming it, because the short, growing hair can irritate the eyes. Leaving the hair at the edges of the eyes long, the same length as the other hair on the head, irritates eyes less. Smooth and comb the hair down and away from the eyes. Curlier hair is harder to tame and may tickle the eyes more

Clean teeth will last longer, and your Havanese's breath will be sweeter, too.

Trimming nails during a bath can speed grooming, but do not let your Havanese get chilled.

often. The more the eyes are irritated, the more they will tear.

You can remove tear stains under the eyes with special products for that purpose. Use a flea comb and cotton ball to remove matter from the inner corners of the eyes. If the matter has dried, use a moistened cotton ball to remove it.

Dental Care

Dental care is important for all dogs but especially for toy dogs whose teeth should last for a long life. Toy dogs have more dental problems because of their smaller mouths, and they tend to lose teeth with age, so good care is critical. Healthy teeth also help avoid bad breath.

Plan on weekly teeth cleaning. Use a small, soft toothbrush and special toothpaste for dogs. In a pinch, a clean, dry washcloth wrapped around your finger can be used to wipe your dog's teeth. Provide your dog with toy dog–sized chew toys and bones that help keep teeth clean and gums healthy. Make sure he cannot chew off a piece and swallow it.

Include a dental exam in your weekly grooming sessions. Look for gums that are a different color than normal, loose teeth, and tartar buildup. Point these out to your veterinarian on your next visit. If puppy teeth do not fall out when adult teeth come in, the puppy teeth may have to be pulled.

Regular nail care will keep the quick from growing too long.

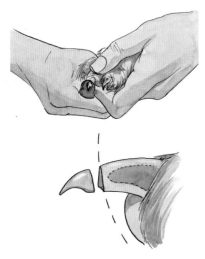

Trim your dog's nails as close to the quick as possible without cutting into the quick.

Nail Care

Long toenails are easy to ignore on coated dogs since the hair covers the nails. Long nails cause the dog to rock back on his feet and splay his toes. If you can hear your dog's nails click on hard floors, they are much too long.

If you let the nails get long, the quick will grow out into the nail. The quick includes blood vessels that supply the nail, and when cut, it bleeds a lot. If you trim your dog's nails regularly, you can keep the quick from growing out.

Plan on trimming your dog's nails every one or two weeks. You can use a clipper or grinder. Clippers come in two styles, scissors and guillotine. Grinders are electric tools that "file" your dog's nails when they are held against a small, spinning sanding drum. No dog likes having his nails cut. Even with the sound of the motor, most tolerate the grinder better than the clippers. When acclimating a dog to the grinder, shorten the hind nails first. Be sure to keep the dog's head up and away from the grinder when working on the front feet. Make short, quick passes with the grinder. Do not allow the grinder to stay in one spot for more than a few seconds as the surface can get very hot.

Hold the coat out of the way when you are working on the nails, especially if you are working with a grinder. Trim each nail, using the tool of your choice, to just short of the quick. If your dog has white nails, you can see the pink quick and easily avoid it. If he has dark nails, look on the underside of the nail and see the nail-only portion that you want to cut or grind off. Remember to clip the dewclaws if your dog has them. These are vestigial toes on the inside of the leg above the paw; some breeders remove them.

Have styptic powder ready to stop the bleeding in case you accidentally cut into the quick.

When trimming around the foot, keep the dog standing to get the correct shape.

In an emergency, you can use unflavored gelatin in place of styptic to stop bleeding.

The easiest way to trim a puppy's nails is to have someone hold him up while you cut the nails. Even when he is older, he can more easily be controlled when wrapped in a bath towel with the foot you are working on protruding.

If you do not want to trim your dog's nails yourself, have your groomer or veterinarian do it. Just make sure you do it at least twice a month. Make sure that she trims them as short as possible without cutting into the quick. Just

TIP

Multitasking During Bath Time

Bath time is a good time to trim your Havanese's nails; they are softened with the water and soap. It is also a good time to clean his ears since the shampoo washes away any debris produced during ear cleaning.

taking off the tips with the nails getting longer and longer is almost as bad as not trimming them at all.

Your big choice is deciding if you will cut your Havanese's coat or if you will use a groomer. If you decide to do it yourself, your breeder or a book or video on grooming can provide the instruction. If you use a groomer, describe the style you want in detail to her. If possible, bring a picture or sketch of the Havanese haircut that you want. Except for the show coat, there are no consistent names for different trims. Do not assume that the groomer will mean the same thing as you do by the phrase "puppy trim."

Coat Trimming

If you want to trim your Havanese's coat yourself, you will need good scissors and/or an electric clipper. Use rounded or blunt-tipped scissors for working around the face. Trim

Trim the hair around the foot and between the pads for safety.

the coat around the feet and the hairs extending between the pads for both cleanliness and safety.

Some trimming is done for cleanliness and hygiene. On males, a semicircle of coat in front of the penis should be clipped to the skin, leaving the hair on the sheath. This keeps urine from getting on the belly coat. The hair left on the penile sheath acts as a wick for the urine. For girls, trim around the lower half of the vulva for cleanliness. On both, trim around the anus and on the inside of the rear legs for better hygiene.

Mats

The Havanese coat will mat and tangle if not brushed often and correctly. Curly coats will mat more often than the desired wavy coat. A puppy coat changing to an adult coat will mat the most. Wet coats will mat if not brushed, combed, and dried—even if just damp from morning dew. Brushing just the topcoat or not thoroughly grooming the dog's armpits or behind the ears is asking for mats. If your dog scratches an itch, due to fleas, allergies, or skin infections, mats may result.

Avoiding mats is a huge incentive to groom your Havanese regularly, to dry off

coats that get wet, and to correct any problem that causes him to scratch. Sometimes, though, mats still happen.

Tools and products such as mat splitters, combs, or rakes help you break up a mat with minimum coat damage. Liquid tangle removers can be used as a conditioner and to help remove tangles. If you find a mat, hold it up and gently pull the hairs at the edges away from the mat. Repeating this process may be adequate to remove the mat. If necessary, saturate the mat with the liquid tangle remover. Work it into the mat, and then leave it until nearly dry. You can use the mat splitter or rake to break the mat into smaller pieces. With your fingers, brush, or comb, gently untangle the hairs until you can brush or comb through them.

Show Coat

You might choose to keep your Havanese in a show coat. This style involves the least trimming. However, since the coat is long, it requires the most care and regular brushing.

The show hairstyle calls for "a profuse mantle of untrimmed long, silky, wavy hair" with a "plumed tail." The coat is not parted down the back. Allowable trimming includes around the feet and pads and around the anal and genital areas for cleanliness. Trimming can also be done on the male's testicles to avoid any mats in that tender area. The hair on the head is not trimmed. Hair at the inside corner of the eyes may be trimmed for hygienic reasons, but doing so is not recommended. The hair may be kept out of the eyes with two braids, one about the outside corner of each eye.

Modified Show Coat

If you love the look, you can keep your Havanese in full coat. You may want to keep the hair out of his eyes, though. When not in the show ring, you can gather the coat into a topknot secured with a cotton-covered elastic band or clip. If you are not showing your dog, you can trim the coat on his head to keep it out of his eyes.

Puppy Trim

This hairstyle has the coat cut to a more manageable length while still maintaining enough coat to look like a Havanese. The feet, anal area, and genital area are still trimmed for safety and good hygiene. The body coat is trimmed to 1 to 2 inches (2.5 to 5 cm). The leg coat is trimmed with some coat left on all sides of the legs. The tail coat is left natural or shortened somewhat.

The coat on the head can be left long enough to gather in a topknot or can be cut short above the eyes so that it does not fall over the eyes. Dogs seem to prefer topknots not be centered on the skull. They fuss with it less when rakishly placed off-center. The ears are trimmed at about the lower jaw level. Enough coat is left on the muzzle to retain the Havanese expression and trimmed about even with the bottom of the ears. This style is also sometimes called the teddy bear trim.

Alternative Puppy Trim

With this style, the coat is cut to the same length all over. The coat can be fairly short,

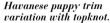

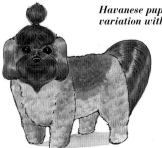

Havanese puppy trim variation with topknot.

Havanese puppy trim variation trimmed short all over.

which is the easiest to care for, or it can be cut to 4 or 5 inches (10 to 12.5 cm) all over. The longer cut will take more care, but it looks the most like a show Havanese.

Coat Type

Remember that a wavy coat is the easiest type of coat to care for, regardless of its length or style of trim. The correct wavy coat will remain attractive and free of mats even if the dog carrying it is groomed less frequently. You might want to select a style based on coat type.

When it gets long, the curly coat tends to mat frequently. Therefore, if your Havanese is curly-coated, you may wish to keep him in a relatively shorter, more-easily managed trim. The curly hair will also curl more when cut short and will come to resemble the coat of a Poodle or a Bichon Frise.

HEALTH CONSIDERATIONS

You can do much to promote good health for your Havanese. Verify the good health of her parents and that they have been health tested for conditions found in the breed. Provide good care, including good nutrition and problem prevention when available. Find a good veterinarian. Understand and learn to recognize those conditions that may affect Havanese.

Finding a Good Veterinarian

Find your veterinarian before you need him, before you get your dog. Veterinarians vary in their levels of expertise and experience. Identify one who is very knowledgeable about toy dogs, especially Havanese. The more he knows, the more accurate his diagnoses will be and the more effective your dog's treatment. How do you find this medical paragon?

If you live near your Havanese's breeder, consider using the veterinarian he uses. If your breeder and his veterinarian are not nearby, find veterinarians used by show dog breeders and owners, especially those with Havanese or

Your Havanese will depend on you to select a knowledgeable veterinarian.

other toy dogs. People with show dogs usually have more dogs and use their veterinarians' services more often.

Your breeder may know other Havanese owners in your area. The HCA has members throughout the country, so check the HCA web site. Your local kennel club, which you can find on the AKC's web site, has members who may help you. Go to shows in your area. The shows, dates, and locations should be on the AKC's web site. Ask local owners of Havanese and other toy dogs which veterinarians they use.

Visit the veterinarians recommended by multiple people. Tell them that you are getting a Havanese. Ask what advice they have to keep your dog in good health. Ask about health issues that affect Havanese and what the

Books on canine health can help you decide when to call your veterinarian.

An eye with a cataract will look cloudy.

recommended treatments are. Inquire about how they handle emergencies since dogs invariably get sick at night and on weekends. Most veterinarians today do not handle their own emergencies if an emergency clinic is available.

Select a veterinarian who has the competence you want and with whom you have the best rapport, one who explains things to you and listens to what you say. Remember that the best veterinarian may not be the one closest to your home. Finding the best veterinarian that you can is worth the extra trouble. The payoff is a healthier Havanese!

Health Issues

The Havanese Club of America lists several health issues that may occur in the breed. These include cataracts, orthopedic or skeletal problems, liver function problems, heart problems, and deafness. This list does not mean the problems are rampant, but you should be aware of them when talking with a breeder and caring for your Havanese.

Cataracts and CERF

A cataract is an opacity of the lens of the eye. Cataracts can be hereditary. They can occur in young and old Havanese. Although they

Curved forearms are characteristic of chondrodysplasia.

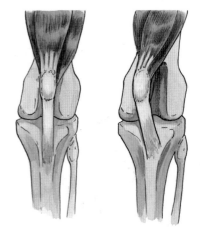

The knee joint on the left is normal; the one on the right illustrates a luxating patella.

restrict vision, they may or may not lead to blindness. They can affect one or both eyes. Correcting cataracts with surgery may offer the best chance of success, and correcting them earlier is preferable to later.

All Havanese should have their eyes examined annually by a canine ophthalmologist to check for eye problems. This exam is often called a CERF exam, for Canine Eye Registry Foundation. The exam results can be registered with CERF. You can confirm that your puppy's parents are current with their CERF exams by checking to see if they are listed on *www.vmdb.org,* the CERF web site.

Your Havanese can develop several different orthopedic problems. Information is presented in this section so you can make informed decisions when obtaining and caring for your Havanese—not to scare you from adopting a member of this very special breed. According to the OFA's web site, well over 90 percent of the

Havanese evaluate normal for the orthopedic conditions tested.

Chondrodysplasia occurs when growth plates of the long bones close (stop growing) earlier than normal. Legs become bowed, twisted, shorter than normal, or different lengths. If the condition is mild, the dog will be able to function. In some dwarf breeds, such as Dachshunds and Basset Hounds, the short, somewhat curved forelegs typical of chondroplasia, are considered normal. Severe cases, which can be painful, may require surgery to straighten the leg. This can be done when the dog is about a year old and skeletal growth is completed.

Luxating patellas: Kneecaps or patellas sit in a groove at the end of the thighbone and are held in place by ligaments. If the patella slips out of the groove, it is luxating. The condition can vary from mild to severe. The more severe conditions cause pain and difficulty moving, and they may be corrected by surgery.

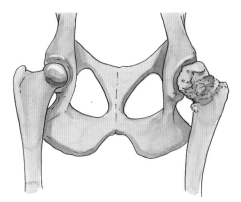

The hip joint on the left is normal; the one on the right is affected by Legg-Calvé-Perthes.

Since the condition may be hereditary, all Havanese should be tested for this condition before being bred. If the patellas are evaluated to be normal, the dogs can be registered and listed with the Orthopedic Foundation for Animals (OFA) as having normal patellas.

Legg-Calvé-Perthes is the reformation (remodeling) or breaking down of the head of the femur (thighbone) that fits into the hip socket. It occurs because the blood supply to the femoral head is inadequate. The dog will be lame and in pain. Surgical correction is available to remove the affected bone and should

The hip joint on the left is normal; the one on the right is affected by Legg-Calvé-Perthes.

relieve the pain. Following surgery, a false joint forms that allows the dog to function approximately normally.

Elbow and hip dysplasia: Elbow dysplasia refers to any of several malformations in the elbow joint. The elbow joint is formed by the juncture of three bones from the upper and lower arms. Problems are caused by improper growth or shape of the bones, by the bones growing at different rates, or by an injury that affects bone growth. In Havanese, chondrodysplasia can also contribute.

Most elbow joint problems occur as the puppy grows. They can be mild to severe, depending on how much change occurs in the bones. Surgery may be called for in more serious cases, but treatments are available that your veterinarian can recommend to reduce inflammation and pain and lubricate the joint. A dog can be x-rayed to determine elbow dysplasia. If she is normal, her clearance can be registered with the OFA and her evaluation listed on the OFA web site.

The hip joint is a ball-and-socket joint. The head of the femur or thighbone is the ball that fits into the socket or acetabulum of the pelvis. When the head of the femur or the socket is misshapen or if the two fit poorly, the dog has hip dysplasia.

A dog with hip dysplasia may have no symptoms at all. Other dogs may be more seriously

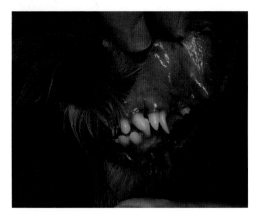

If your veterinarian finds a puppy canine tooth retained when the adult tooth grows in, the puppy tooth can be pulled.

Your veterinarian will listen to your Havanese's heart during her annual exam.

affected. The condition usually gets progressively worse as the dog ages, with arthritic changes in the imperfectly formed and fitting joint.

The cause of hip dysplasia is unknown, but it has a hereditary component. Although not a big problem with Havanese, some breeders have their dogs' hips evaluated by OFA or PennHip so they can reduce the risk of hip dysplasia in their puppies. Parents that test clear may produce an offspring with hip problems.

Portosystemic Shunt

Havanese may have a liver abnormality called a portosystemic shunt. It is a condition where the blood that would normally flow through the liver is shunted around it. The majority of liver shunts are congenital—75 percent, and symptoms are seen when the dog is a young puppy. Symptoms include loss of appetite, weakness, poor balance, and disorientation. The puppies tend to be smaller than their littermates and do not thrive. The condition is fatal if not treated when toxins build up. If the shunt is simple, it may be corrected by surgery. Dietary and medical management of the condition may be possible for some dogs.

Heart Problems

Heart murmurs have been found in Havanese. It is usually caused by a weakening of a heart valve. It can lead to more problems, such as heart failure, if left untreated. Drugs and diet changes may be prescribed, and your veterinarian may consider surgery.

Deafness

Deafness can occur in one or both ears of a Havanese. It can be identified in puppies as young as five weeks. Deafness is determined

An annual physical includes examination of the eyes, ears, and mouth.

Finding fleas or ticks on a Havanese with a dark coat is a challenge.

with a test called the BAER (brain audio evoked response) test. Results can be registered with the OFA. One BAER test is sufficient to determine hearing; it need not be repeated during the dog's life.

External Parasites

Fleas and ticks are the most common external parasites. They are annoying, cause skin problems, and carry disease. They are especially big problems for your coated dog, for she will scratch and produce mats. If your dog has these parasites, you must simultaneously treat the dog, your home, and your yard.

Flea collars can be used on Havanese, but do not let mats form under the collar. You can also keep a flea collar in your vacuum cleaner bag. Topical products available from your veterinarian are effective, including imidacloprid (Advantage) and fipronil (Frontline), which spread to cover the dog and kill the parasites when they get on the dog. When treating the house and yard, make sure to use a product that kills the adult fleas and ticks and also the eggs. Otherwise, in two weeks, you will have a new infestation.

Finding fleas and ticks is a challenge on the longer coat of your Havanese, especially on dark-colored coats. A flea comb is useful for isolating the fleas. When looking for ticks, make sure you examine inside and behind your dog's ears, where her legs join her body, and on her feet between her toes. Look and feel through the coat in order to locate ticks.

Internal Parasites

Internal parasites are primarily intestinal worms: hookworms, tapeworms, roundworms, and whipworms. When a dog has any of these worms, your veterinarian can often detect them by examining a stool sample under a microscope. You may be able to see bits of white tapeworm (about 0.25 to 0.5 inches [0.6 to 1.3 cm] in length) in your dog's stool.

Intestinal worms: If your Havanese has diarrhea, have her checked for worms and infection. Intestinal worms are usually easily treatable. Pick up and dispose of your dog's feces to help avoid spreading worms. Have your

Take your Havanese for an annual physical exam even if she is vaccinated less frequently.

dog's stool examined as part of her yearly health check-up.

Heartworm: If mosquitoes are in your area, your Havanese must be on heartworm preventive. When mosquitoes carrying heartworm bite your dog, the heartworm larvae are transmitted to the dog. The larvae develop in the body and grow to adult heartworms in the dog's heart and lungs. They eventually kill the dog.

Although heartworm can be treated, doing so is expensive and hard on the dog. A far better alternative is to give your dog regular heartworm prevention medicine. There are a variety of options for heartworm prevention, including monthly tablets, chewables, and topicals. They are extremely effective. When they are administered on schedule, heartworm infection is completely avoidable. A Havanese who is not on heartworm preventative must be checked for heartworms before starting it.

An Ounce of Prevention

Diseases that killed dogs a few decades ago can now be prevented by the use of vaccines. Your Havanese puppy will have gotten her initial vaccines while with her breeder. On her first visit to your veterinarian, take the record of the inoculations she has had so far. Your veterinarian will recommend a series of vaccines and when they should be administered. Puppy vaccines are usually given at three- to four-week intervals.

Good care and good parents contribute to a good long life.

Vaccines are categorized as core and noncore. The core vaccines protect against diseases that are very serious and potentially fatal. They include canine parvovirus, canine distemper virus, canine adenovirus, and rabies. Noncore vaccines are for diseases that are less serious, easily treated, self-limiting, or that your puppy has little risk of contracting. They include canine parainfluenza virus, distemper-measles combination, bordatella, leptospirosis, and Lyme disease. Many owners are now inoculating only with the core vaccines, including noncore vaccines only when their dogs will have significant exposure.

Traditionally, vaccines were administered annually to boost the dog's immunity. Many vaccines available now for adult dogs provide three-year immunity. Giving inoculations less often reduces the chance of vaccine reactions. Some feel that Havanese are sensitive to vaccines, and so they do not give all the vaccines in a single combined shot and do not give the rabies shot at the same time as the others. Discuss with your veterinarian what vaccines to give and how often. Even if you use three-year vaccines, see your veterinarian annually for your Havanese's checkup.

Senior Citizens

Havanese life expectancy averages from 14 to 15 years. With luck and good care, yours may well live longer. As your dog ages, you will notice that she is less active. An older dog's pigment may lighten, and her skin may be dry and itch more. You may see small skin tumors and skin tags that accompany aging. Some loss of hearing and vision and arthritis occur in senior Havanese. Your dog may have tooth and gum problems, making it uncomfortable to eat.

As your Havanese ages, monitor her condition. Continue regular veterinarian visits. Get a senior exam, including blood tests, to determine that her organs are functioning properly. Have her eyes, mouth, and teeth checked.

Your older dog's diet may need to be modified. She may need fewer calories but will still need quality protein to keep her body in good repair. If she has problems with her teeth, softer food will be easier for her to eat. Continue to clean her teeth regularly, because they will not stay as clean with soft food. She may need a special diet you can get from your veterinarian if some of her organs are not functioning properly.

Time to Say Good-bye

At some point, it will be time to say good-bye to your Havanese. Although not pleasant, it is the final gift you can give her in return for all the love she has given you.

Deciding when to do it can be hard. It should be determined by the quality of life the dog has. She does not have to be as athletic as a youngster to have a quality life. If she enjoys the warmth of the sun, being near you, getting a cookie, and is not in much pain, she has a good life. When pain from disease or age is substantial enough to prevent any pleasure, though, the time has come. Your veterinarian can help you decide.

The other big decision is the final resting place for your dog. You can bury your Havanese on your property or in a pet cemetery. If you choose to bury her at home, you need to check if local codes allow this. In addition, remember that you may move someday. Many people leave their dogs at the veterinarian, not knowing that a mass grave or a landfill may be the final resting place. Consider cremation, available through many veterinary practices. You may keep the ashes, bury, or scatter them (again, if local codes allow). If you keep them, perhaps on some high shelf in your home, your Havanese will be as close as she still is in your heart.

If your dog won't get up, he may be sick.

An observant owner is critical to a dog's health. Notice changes that might indicate a problem. Write down everything you see to tell your veterinarian. You know your dog best and what is normal for her. You will see subtle changes that your veterinarian may miss. The doctor depends on you for this vital information.

Standing, Moving, and Energy

Notice any differences in her posture, movement, or activity. Her energy level may change; her mood may be altered. She may limp, be stiff, or be uncoordinated. She may have trouble breathing. She may stand tensed, head hanging, body hunched up.

What Goes In and What Comes Out

Look for changes in her eating or drinking habits. Is she urinating more or less frequently? Are there changes in her stool or the frequency of defecation? Is there any blood in her urine or stool? Is she vomiting? If so, what comes up?

Body Changes

When you groom your Havanese, notice any lumps, bumps, or abrasions. Are there changes in her coat? Is it dry, falling out, or a different texture? Does the body feel the same on both sides? Is any area sensitive or tender? If your male is intact, confirm that his testicles feel the same, have not changed in size or firmness, and are approximately the same size. See if discharge is coming from any orifice.

Allergies

Is your Havanese itching? Does she scratch herself frequently or rub herself with vigor against fences or furni-ture? Does she lick or chew at herself? A light-colored coat that is repeatedly licked can change color as the digestive juices in the saliva will chemically change the hairs. Are her eyes red or weepy? Dogs can develop allergies to plants, grasses, dander, pollen, fleas, dust, molds, and foods.

If you see any or all of these behaviors in your dog, have your Havanese evaluated by a veterinary dermatologist. There are many ways an allergic dog can be helped.

Ears and Teeth

Check your dog's mouth regularly for sore gums and loose or painful teeth. Check her ears regularly for infections or parasites, such as fleas, ticks, or ear mites. If your Havanese paws at, or scratches her ears or muzzle, she might have a problem to identify and correct.

Taking Temperature

If you suspect your dog might be ill, take her temperature. Shake down a rectal thermometer to about 95°F (35°C). Lubricate the tip with petroleum jelly, and insert it about an inch (2.5 cm) into the anus. Hold it there for about three minutes, and then take it out, and read it. Normal canine temperature is 101 to 102°F (38.3 to 38.9°C). If her tempera-

A healthy Havanese is happy and lively, walks and runs comfortably, and eagerly greets the world.

ture is 1°F (0.5°C) higher or lower, call your veterinarian. If it is more than 2°F (1°C) above or below normal, take her to a veterinarian right away.

OFA (Orthopedic Foundation for Animals)

OFA's web site at *www.offa.org* lists the Havanese that are registered for any of several conditions. OFA registers and reports dogs' evaluations for hip dysplasia, elbow dysplasia, cardiac exams, CERF eye tests, Legg-Calvé-Perthes, patellas, BAER hearing test, and many others. You can check this site to see what health tests your puppy's parents have had.

First Aid Kit

Some over-the-counter products are useful to have. Before administering one, ask your veterinarian about whether to give it to your dog and, if so, what dose to use. Include sterile gauze pads, self-adhesive bandages, antibiotic ointment, antidiarrhea medicine, eye ointment, hydrogen peroxide, baby aspirin, and upset stomach medicine. You can also include unflavored gelatin that can be used in an emergency to stop bleeding.

Check your kit monthly to see if any items have expired. If so, throw them out immediately and replace them with fresh items just as quickly.

Rubbing Alcohol

Rubbing alcohol is toxic to both fleas and ticks. If you find a flea on your dog, spray it with rubbing alcohol. If you find a tick attached to your dog, spray it with alcohol first to loosen its grip. Grab it next to the dog's skin with tweezers, pull it off, and drop it into a bit of alcohol.

Giving Medicine

Wrap a pill in soft cheese, meat, or peanut butter, which should be sufficient inducement to get your Havanese to take the pill. You can also open her mouth and put the pill at the far back

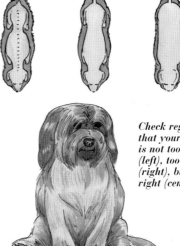

Check regularly that your dog is not too thin (left), too plump (right), but just right (center).

of her mouth. Hold her mouth closed, and stroke her throat until she swallows.

Liquid medicine can most easily be given with a syringe. Remove the needle. Draw the liquid into the syringe. Put the syringe inside your dog's cheek toward the back of her mouth. Hold her muzzle closed and tipped slightly up, and squirt the liquid into the back of her mouth.

Health Survey

HCA surveyed Havanese owners on the health of their dogs. Health survey results are available on *www.havanese.org*, the HCA web site. Link to the survey data from the Havanese health web page. It is a great resource for information.

After a Veterinarian Visit

After visiting your veterinarian, watch your Havanese closely to see if she is responding to the treatment and medication prescribed. If she is not, tell your veterinarian and schedule another visit. Do not just wait and hope the dog will get better.

TRAINING AND RECREATION

Your Havanese has been learning since the day he was born, and you will be involved in his education from the day he arrives at your home. He is very intelligent and wants to be with and please you, which makes him relatively easy to train. Remember that he is not a mind reader, though, and you must help him understand what you want.

Housebreaking

Plan to spend 100 percent of your time initially establishing patterns and habits you want your Havanese to use for elimination. Decide the place in your yard you want him to use. If you have a doggy door, he can go out by himself. However, you will have to teach him how to use it. Some toy dog owners also make a potty station in the house within the area the dog can get to. You can use dog litter, similar to cat litter, or pee pads, which are made of material similar to disposable diapers. Make sure the pee pad is secured (plastic frames are available for this), or your puppy may shred it.

The spot: You must get your puppy to the potty place when he needs to go, which means

Your bright Havanese is ready for fun and adventure each day.

you have to anticipate. Take him there immediately when he wakes up, after eating or drinking, and when he sniffs the ground during play. You have only a second or two, so you will have to be alert and fast.

Using a crate can help, because your puppy will not want to soil his bed. He will make a little fuss that will give you an extra couple of seconds to get him to the proper place. When he performs his duty, praise him calmly and give him a tiny treat. Limiting your dog's access in the house and using exercise pens (ex-pens) and baby gates also helps. The younger and less trained the dog, the smaller the area he should have access to. You can put his food and water on a schedule; what goes in on time tends to come out on time.

Prevention: The idea is to prevent as many accidents as possible. Dogs are creatures of habit. If you get them into the habit of potty-ing in a certain place, they will want to return to that place the next time nature calls.

If an accident does happen and you catch him in process, interrupt him, say "No," take him to the correct place, and then praise him. Never correct the dog if the accident has already happened. He will not associate the correction with the accident.

A device for male dogs is a belly band. You can buy one into which an absorbent pad is inserted, or you can use a disposable diaper.

A pen and gates can confine your Havanese during housebreaking.

It goes around the dog's waist, over his penis, and is taped or tied at his back. Then, if he uri-nates, it goes into the pad. (Take the belly band off when you take him outside.)

Toy dogs have smaller capacities than big dogs, need to go more often, and are therefore harder to housebreak. If you are persistent and consistent, he can be reliably housebroken by about six to seven months of age.

How Dogs Learn

Before you can effectively train your dog, you need to know how dogs learn. Basically, dogs do what feels good and avoid what feels bad. What you want them to do must feel good, and you do this by rewarding them.

One reward is petting and praising your dog. This is fine, but would you work only for pet-ting and praise? Probably not; you would want something more tangible. For your dog, the reward is food. Extraspecial, wonderfully tasty food is much higher octane than plain dog bis-cuits. Find what food your dog really, really loves, and use that as the reward for doing what you want. Meat is often a good choice, as is cheese.

Use the treat to shape the behavior you want, to entice the dog to come, sit, or lie down, without touching him if possible. When he does it or comes close, give him the treat. As he learns, treat him for the better perform-ances. When he gets reliable, you can reinforce him intermittently, which is the most effective reinforcement. Always tell him what a good boy he is, pet him, and praise him.

Keep the training sessions short, frequent, and fun. Always leave him wanting more. Ten three-minute sessions are better than one half-hour session. Get a treat, have him sit, give him the treat, and praise. Then go do something else.

Naming the behavior: Most people use the command to teach a dog to do something, knowing that the dog does not know the word. Teach the behavior first with the treat, and then attach the word to it. Hold the treat above his head to get him to sit. When he is doing it reliably, then say *"Sit"* when offering the treat. Eventually, he will connect hearing *"Sit"* with the behavior he is already doing and will do it for the command.

The thinking dog: You have gotten your Havanese to sit for the treat and commanded *"Sit."* At some point during the learning process, you will command *"Sit"* and hold the treat, but your dog will just stand and look at you. If you have said the command clearly, do not repeat it. Do not put the dog into the *sit* position. Just stand with the offered treat, watch your dog, and wait. The dog wants the treat. He needs to figure out what to do to get it. It may take several minutes, but as long as the dog is thinking, let him do it. It is part of learning. When he figures it out and sits, jackpot! Give him several treats.

Change the context: When your Havanese learns to sit, it is fixed in his mind in the location (e.g., your living room) and your behavior (e.g., standing in front of him). He does not generalize the *sit* to other locations, to your behaving differently, or to someone else saying it. So part of training is to vary the context. Teach him *sit* in the backyard, in the front yard, in the bedroom, in a training class. Teach him *sit* with you standing by his side, behind him, and a few feet in front of him. Teach him to sit with other people and dogs around. As he gets more reliable, add distractions: another dog barking, a child running, a doorbell ringing.

Include children in your Havanese's lessons.

Specific Commands

The most useful commands for a house dog are *sit, down, stay,* and *come*. We discussed teaching *sit* above. Put the treat above his head. As his head comes up to get the treat, his bottom goes down toward the floor. When it

TIP

Housebreaking and Altering

Spaying and neutering your Havanese by six months of age will help with housebreaking. Unaltered dogs that reach sexual maturity are more likely to mark in the house.

TIP

Will Work for Food

Use each meal as a training opportunity by having your Havanese do something for his food. Practice *sit* or *down*. When he knows *sit* and *down*, have him *stay* until you put the food down. Remember to release him with "OK."

hits the floor, give him the treat and lots of praise. When he gets the concept, you can say, *"Sit."*

Down is easiest to teach when the dog is in the sitting position. Starting with the treat in front of your sitting dog's face, bring it down to the floor slowly. His nose should follow the treat to the floor. When his elbows hit the ground, treat and praise. His bottom must stay on the floor, though, for him to be in the *down* position. When he reliably lies down for the treat, you can connect the command, *"Down."*

Stay is a bit different. You are not asking the dog to do something. You are asking him to not do something, to not move. The trick is to progress in tiny increments. Have your dog sit. Put your palm in front of his eyes, and say *"Stay."* Count to 5, tell him "OK" and "Good Boy!" and give him a treat. When he can do that, count to 10. Then 15; then 20. When he can do that reliably, tell him *"Stay"* and take one step away. Since you increased the distance, reduce the length of time back to a count of 5 or 10. Do not increase time and distance at the same time. Gradually increase the time at that distance. When you increase the distance again, ask for the shorter time. Make sure you release him when the *stay* is over; "OK" is a frequently used release word. When you say "OK," he knows he can move.

Come is probably the most valuable and useful command. Crouch down with the treat, and call his name and *"Come."* Use an enthusiastic, high-pitched voice to encourage him. When he comes, pet, praise, and treat him.

Introduce your Havanese to men and women, young and old, at home and away.

Many times a day, at unexpected times, call him to you to get a treat. Coming to you must always, always be a positive, wonderful experience. Never ever call him to do something he does not like—taking a bath, having his nails trimmed, or getting medicine. Never, never, **never** call him to you to correct him for anything. If you do, you are teaching him not to come to you when called.

Nipping

Puppies, like babies, put their mouths onto everything, and they have needle-sharp teeth. Puppies must learn bite inhibition in regards to people.

They have already learned it from their mother and their littermates. If they bite too hard, their mother and siblings let them know about it. Next time in play, they do not bite that hard.

We need to do the equivalent to teach him how much is too much with people. When you play with your puppy and he puts his mouth and teeth onto you or your hair (puppies love hair), say "Ouch" with as much feeling as you can muster, and stop playing. Turn your back on him and go away. Game over. "If you are going to play that way with your mouth," you are telling him, "I am not going to play with you." Do it every time he puts his mouth onto you. He is a fun-loving, social creature and wants to play and be with you. He will quickly learn to stop putting his mouth onto you because it ends his game and his pleasure in your company. Have others do the same so he knows that mouthing any person is not acceptable. Monitor him with children so that you can do the equivalent when he puts his mouth onto a child.

If you teach your dog to stay, you can get some clever photos.

Time for a Walk

Part of the fun of having a Havanese is being able to take him many places with you. It will be more fun if he will walk nicely on a lead. Remember to use a correctly sized collar: not too small but not so large that he can slip it off and run away.

Your puppy will want to go and will pull on the lead. Make a deal with him. If he does not pull on the lead, the walk can continue. Every time he pulls, stop walking and stand still. When he looks back and puts some slack in the lead, start walking again. When the lead is taut again, stop. Resume walking when the lead is slack. He will quickly notice that he gets to go only when the lead is not tight and will modify his behavior to keep the lead loose so the walk can continue. The key is consistency. If the walk continues when he pulls, he will persist in pulling.

Time Alone

Havanese are very social dogs. He wants to be with you, next to you, or on your lap. Since this is not always possible, teach him as a puppy to be alone periodically. After making sure he does not have to go to the bathroom, leave him alone in his crate or ex-pen. Leave the room.

Two smiling faces.

To make being alone more palatable, provide chewies and toys to entertain him. You might leave the radio or television set on for company. Do not respond to his fussing at being alone.

When you return, do not make a big deal of your arrival. Act as if you had not left. Do not pay attention to the dog for a few minutes.

If you are so inclined, other pets are fantastic company for your dog. How about getting another Havanese?

Activities and Events

Now that your Havanese is happy and well behaved, there are many activities you two can enjoy together. More details on the AKC activities can be found on AKC's web site.

Canine Good Citizen

The AKC's Canine Good Citizen (CGC) program rewards dogs that are well behaved. Dogs that pass the CGC test receive a certificate from the AKC. A minimum of obedience training should enable your Havanese to earn his CGC. The test consists of ten steps. The test looks at his behavior with strangers and other dogs, appearance and grooming, walking on a lead, sitting, and coming when called.

Obedience

Obedience clubs offer classes that are excellent places to train your dog and see how far you both want to go in obedience. Train with a class as well as at home. Your dog needs to perform the exercises with other dogs and distractions. You practice at home. However, if your dog obeys only at home, his training is definitely incomplete.

Walking is good exercise for you and your Havanese.

If you liked CGC and want to compete for AKC obedience titles, there are three you can aim for. These have progressive levels of difficulty.

The Companion Dog or CD title can be earned from the novice level class in obedience trials. The novice exercises including heeling, stand for examination by the judge, coming when called, and stays in the *sit* and *down* positions.

The Companion Dog Excellent or CDX title is the goal when competing in open classes. The open exercises include many of the same CD exercises, all off lead, with longer *sits* and *downs*, plus having the dog *down* when he is coming to you, doing retrieves, and going over jumps.

Utility-level dogs compete for a Utility Dog or UD title. The utility class exercises include some of the same CDX exercises, including using hand signals, plus retrieving a dumbbell that you touched, retrieving a glove you point to, and jumping an obstacle you point to.

Rally

Rally is the AKC's newest titling competition event. It builds on obedience exercises. Each dog and handler progress through a course of 10 to 20 stations. Each station tells the pair to do something, such as *sit, down, left turn, call your dog,* and more. The event allows unlimited communication between handler and dog, including multiple commands, praising the dog, and encouraging him but not touching him.

Rally has several levels of classes and titles. The levels vary in the number of stations and the types of exercises at the stations. Rally novice classes are done with the dog on lead. The dog must be off lead for rally advanced and rally excellent classes. The higher-level classes include harder exercises, such as jumps, and more stations. The Rally Advanced Excellent title can be earned after the Rally Excellent title by qualifying 10 times in both the rally advanced and rally excellent classes at the same competitions.

A dog who will **Down** *and* **Stay** *shows good manners and is a welcomed guest.*

TIP

Come!

According to trainers, "Havanese are 'runners' who love to just take off." Do not expect your dog to stay close by off lead naturally. This makes the *come* command especially important. Reinforce it every day, several times a day when possible, in many different situations. In addition, do not give your Havanese the opportunity to run off.

Agility

Agility is one of the most popular and fastest growing AKC events. At agility trials, dogs run through a timed obstacle course. The goal is to run the course within the standard time with the fewest faults. The obstacles include the A-frame, the dog walk (an elevated board that the dog must walk across), the seesaw, the pause table, a variety of jumps, the weave poles, and tunnels.

The three levels of competition are called novice, open, and excellent. Each has a different number of obstacles on the course and vary

Dogs offer children unconditional love and acceptance and teach them to be caring and responsible.

in the amount of handling or teamwork expected between you and your dog. The courses can also vary with the obstacles included. The standard course may include all the obstacles. In contrast, jumpers with weaves excludes the contact obstacles, those where the dog must touch a certain part of the obstacle. Preferred classes are offered with slightly lower jump heights and longer standard times.

If your dog gets a qualifying score, he earns a leg toward his title. Many titles are available in agility, based on the combination of level, type of course, and preferred or not. Agility is open to all AKC breeds, but the obstacles do not change size for the different breeds beyond varying the jump heights. Some can be a challenge for a small dog. If you and your Havanese like it, it is great fun.

Therapy Dogs

Your Havanese is social and loves people. If you are so inclined, you can share him with others who love but have no access to dogs. He can be a therapy dog.

Therapy dogs visit people in care facilities that are receptive to dogs, bringing friendship, entertainment, and memories of dogs the people have had. It has been proven that dogs improve people's quality of life and health, and a Havanese is temperamentally well suited to bringing that to people.

Therapy dogs visit nursing homes, assisted-living facilities, children's homes, and other

institutions that welcome dogs. If schools are receptive, they can visit schools to help teach children about responsible dog ownership. Dogs are now participating in reading programs,

Your lively Havanese will enjoy the jumps in obedience and agility.

Even a cute Havanese can have a bad hair day.

where children read to dogs and learn to read more confidently.

Multiple organizations register therapy dogs and provide guidance to participants. They test the dogs to insure that they are adequately trained and personally suited to be therapy dogs. Often several dogs in the same organization will visit a site as a group.

Some organizations that register therapy dogs are national; others are regional or local. Some of the national groups are Therapy Dogs International, Therapy Dogs Inc., Delta Society, and Love on a Leash.

Show Time!

At dog shows, Havanese can compete for their conformation championship. It is called conformation because the dogs are evaluated on how closely they conform to or resemble the perfect Havanese as described by the Havanese standard. After examining the dogs standing and moving, a judge awards points to one female and one male she thinks are the best. When a Havanese wins enough points, he can earn his championship.

If you want to compete in dog shows, tell your breeder that you want a show-potential puppy. She will help you select one than can be competitive at dog shows. Training for dog shows is not difficult. Your dog must stand on a grooming table and let the judge go over him. He must also trot in a straight line on lead next to you.

A dog entered in a dog show must be intact, that is, not spayed or neutered. A Havanese must also have its long coat. Showing your dogs, therefore, means a commitment to coat grooming. It is one more fun activity you can share together.

Organizations

Note: Officers and contacts will change. Check with the web sites for current contact information.

American Kennel Club
580 Centerview Drive
Raleigh, NC 27606-3390
(919) 233-9767
www.akc.org

Havanese Club of America
www.havanese.org
E-mail: secy@havanese.org

Havanese Club of Great Britain
www.havaneseclub.co.uk

Havanese Fanciers of Canada
www.havanesefanciers.com

Magazines

AKC Gazette
General dog and multibreed magazine. Contact the AKC for subscription information.

The Havanese Hotline
The official publication of the HCA and available to members. Contact the HCA regarding membership.

Books

Braund, Kathryn, *The Joyous Havanese*, Kathryn Braund Publications, Great Falls, MT, 2005.
Donaldson, Jean, *Culture Clash,* James & Kenneth Publishers, Berkley, CA, 1997.
Goodale, Dorothy, *Havanese, A Complete and Reliable Handbook*, T.F.H. Publications Inc., Neptune City, NJ, 2000.

Guerra, Zoila Portuondo, Translated by Jane McManus, *Bichon Havanese*, Pet Love, Surrey, England (distributor), Animalia, Hong Kong, China: (copyright), 1999.

Health Web Sites

BAER (Brain Audio Evoked Response) Test Sites
www.lsu.edu/deafness/baersite.htm

CERF (Canine Eye Registry Foundation)
www.vmdb.org

OFA (Orthopedic Foundation for Animals)
www.offa.org

A well-groomed Havanese in a short tidy hairdo.

INDEX

About the Author

Nikki Riggsbee is an award-winning author of multiple articles and books directed at both pet owners and the dog showing public. She has had dogs all of her life, has shown and bred dogs for over twenty-five years, and judges 60 AKC breeds at dog shows. As a breeder, she is particularly interested in prospective owners selecting the right breed for them and having the breed-specific knowledge to take excellent care of their dogs and to provide them with the good lives they deserve. Getting a dog is like adding a member to the family, and it should be a lifelong commitment.

Acknowledgments

The author is sincerely grateful to all the Havanese owners and breeders who shared their dogs and their expertise in this book to benefit other Havanese pet owners. A special thank you goes to those breeders and owners who reviewed the chapters as they were being written and offered additional information. Much appreciation is directed at the folks at Barron's who offered suggestions and fine-tuning, especially to senior editor Seymour Weiss, our project leader who made it all come together.

Important Note

This pet owner's manual tells the reader how to buy or adopt, and care for a Havanese. The author and publisher consider it important to point out that the advice given in the book is meant primarily for normally developed dogs of excellent physical health and sound temperament.

Anyone who acquires a fully-grown dog should be aware that the animal has already formed its basic impressions of human beings. The new owner should observe the animal carefully, including its behavior toward humans, and, whenever possible, should meet the previous owner.

Caution is further advised in the association of children with dogs, in meeting with other dogs, and in exercising the dog without a leash. These matters assume even greater importance when the dog is of a Toy breed.

Even well-behaved and carefully supervised dogs can sometimes damage property or cause accidents. It is therefore in the owner's interest to be adequately insured against such eventualities, and we strongly urge all dog owners to purchase a liability policy that also covers their dog.

Photo Credits

Kent Akselsen: 8, 9, 19, 20, 21, 27, 32 (bottom), 40, 45, 46, 56, 58, 61, 62, 63 (top right and left and bottom), 64 (right), 65 (right), 66, 67, 74, 84, 86, 89, 92, 93; Norvia Behling: 6, 12, 29, 32 (top), 35 (top left), 37, 43, 51, 52, 64 (left), 65, (left) 72, 75 (top and bottom), 82, 85, 88, 90, 91 (top); Kent Dannen: 13, 17, 39, 44, 59; Cheryl Ertelt: 4, 30, 57, 87, 91 (bottom); Pets by Paulette: 2, 5, 6, 10, 11, 14, 18, 22, 23, 24, 25, 26, 28, 33, 34 (top and bottom), 35 (top right and bottom), 36, 38, 48, 49, 53, 55, 70, 71, 78, 79, 83; Connie Summers: 76, 77.

Cover Photos

Norvia Behling: front cover, back cover, and inside back cover; Tara Darling: inside front cover.

All inquiries should be addressed to:
Barron's Educational Series, Inc.
250 Wireless Boulevard
Hauppauge, NY 11788
http://www.barronseduc.com

ISBN-13: 978-0-7641-3389-3
ISBN-10: 0-7641-3389-6
Library of Congress Catalog Card No. 2006042704

Library of Congress Cataloging-in-Publication Data
Riggsbee, Nikki.
    Havanese : everything about purchase, care, nutrition, behavior, and training / Nikki Riggsbee ; illustrations by Michele Earle-Bridges.
        p. cm.
    Includes bibliographical references and index.
    ISBN-13: 978-0-7641-3389-3 (alk. paper)
    ISBN-10: 0-7641-3389-6 (alk. paper)
        1. Havanese dog. I. Earle-Bridges, Michele.
    II. Title.

SF429.H37R54   2006
636.767—dc22   2006042704

Printed in China
9 8 7